INTERGALACTIC WARFARE

Spiritual Warfare between God and the Devil

David Siriano

5 Fold Media
Visit us at www.5foldmedia.com

Intergalactic Warfare: Spiritual Warfare between God and the Devil

Copyright © 2013 by David E. Siriano

Published by 5 Fold Media, LLC

www.5foldmedia.com

ISBN: 978-1-936578-76-4

Library of Congress Control Number: 2013947654

Dedication

To the memory of the late Rev. Dr. Robert Lundstrom (1931-2012), former instructor at Zion Bible College, Valley Forge Christian College, and Trinity Bible College.

He was a friend, scholar, mentor, and prayer partner who gave me numerous opportunities to teach in his prophecy classes on the college level.

We had many discussions about the end times and the events that will take place on the Earth before the return of the Lord Jesus Christ.

Contents

Foreword   7

Introduction   9

Chapter One: How Spiritual Warfare Began   11

IN THE BEGINNING GOD   11

THE CORE OF SPIRITUAL WARFARE   13

THE HUMAN FACTOR IN SPIRITUAL WARFARE   17

LUCIFER   25

ANGELS OF THE HEAVENLY REALM   29

THE DESIGN OF THE "GREAT TRIBULATION"   35

Chapter Two: Men of God and Spiritual Warfare   39

ABRAHAM   39

JACOB   41

MOSES AND THE PASSOVER ANGEL   42

ELIJAH AND THE FALSE PROPHETS   44

JOB   47

PAUL   56

DANIEL   59

DANIEL'S INTERGALACTIC WARFARE   63

EZEKIEL   68

JEREMIAH   70

BIRTH OF JESUS   72

THE TEMPTATION OF JESUS   75

THE GARDEN AND THE CROSS   78

Chapter Three: Why God Uses Prayer and Spiritual Warfare 85

WHY GOD NEEDS PEOPLE TO PRAY   85
MOVING THE HAND OF GOD   89
THE PUZZLING CONCEPT OF PRAYER   95
WHY DOESN'T GOD ANSWER ALL PRAYERS?   102
HOW SATAN GETS A FOOTHOLD   108

Chapter Four: Intercessory Prayer   115

PRINCIPLES FOR EFFECTIVE INTERCESSION   121
A WARNING   125
WAYS TO PRAY FOR PEOPLE IN AUTHORITY   127

Chapter Five: Why Nations Go To War   131

WHERE HAS GOD BEEN?   131
GOD IS IN CONTROL OF THE WORLD   132
THE LAND OF CANAAN (PALESTINE)   136
ISRAEL OR THE CHURCH   144
YOU MUST GET THESE THINGS RIGHT   151
THE PURPOSE OF SUPERPOWERS   155
THE CONSEQUENCES OF WAR   162

Chapter Six: God and the Future   171

INTERVENTION BY GOD   171
WHAT ABOUT THE FUTURE?   174
OH LORD, SEND A REVIVAL   176
CHAOS AND THE RETURN OF JESUS CHRIST   180
PRAYER FOR THE NATIONS   191

Foreword

There are a number of books that have been written about spiritual warfare. They are all designed to try and help the reader understand the difficulty in dealing with the Devil and his army of demonic spirits. They deal with the personal battles in the spiritual realms that affect the reader as he or she grapples with these sinister forces.

There are some who believe that demons have to be cast out of those with certain disabilities such as fear, emotional problems, mental illnesses, physical deformities, schizophrenia, nervous disorders, and other physical sicknesses. While demons can be associated with these issues that oppress us or bind us as revealed in the Bible, not all of them are of the nature of demon possession. Matthew 4:23-25 and Mark 1:32-34 seem to make the distinction between those with serious diseases and those who were demon possessed.

There are some who try to get us to renounce the works of the Devil, the occult, false religions, bondages, and addictions. Their attention never seems to move from the personal problems that each of us face on a small and local conflict level; they never lift the eyes of the reader to the real battle in the heavens far above this earthly domain where the real spiritual warfare is taking place. This is where many writers and readers get it wrong!

Writers may mention the heavenly battles and the implications of the startling conflict of the ages, but they never seem to really get to it. They refer to the powerful movements of the nations of history, but never expand on them. They always seem to come back to the personal and human factor of fighting in spiritual warfare.

Intergalactic Warfare

Usually when we think of spiritual warfare, we apply it to our own personal lives and our daily living. We want to know how we can improve ourselves by fighting and winning over the forces of this life that affect us in our everyday struggles.

That is not what this book is about. This book is about trying to understand the great cosmic battles between those powers of the universe that war on the side of God against the powers of the universe that war on the side of the Devil. It deals with the core of what spiritual warfare is really about: the spiritual warfare between God and the Devil.

While spiritual warfare affects our Christian walk on a day-by-day basis, we should lift our eyes to the principalities and powers that are warring with each other—and get our eyes off of how they are warring with us. It means gaining an intergalactic praying and thinking perspective. It means warring over territories in the Spirit realm that affect the entire universe, and not just our personal territories with which we are familiar. Doing this can change our world.

I want us to take a look at spiritual warfare as warfare of gigantic proportions that has a tremendous impact on the nations of the world. In the future, God will bring this world to a startling conclusion as Jesus Christ returns to this earth to bring an end to human history.

God's spiritual warfare over the nations as we approach the end times, including the great tribulation and the battle of Armageddon, is the focus of this book.

Introduction

We generally think very narrowly and we do not see the entire scope of spiritual warfare. Most of us look at it as fighting the power of the Devil as he attempts to thwart many of our personal activities here on earth. Many try to deal with the battles of personal injustices we have in regard to our activities and circumstances—our jobs, our positions, our family's salvation and protection, our pensions, our debts, or other things that affect us economically as we fight and wrestle for our own personal fortune.

We say that we have fought with the Devil to gain victory for ourselves. This is all well and good, but there is something about spiritual warfare that should involve more than just our own personal interests. At stake are things even greater than our own personal circumstances. We need to rise to the core of spiritual warfare in order to get to the root of the battle.

God wants us to look beyond the horizon of our surroundings and look to the heavens of conflict. He wants us to understand what this conflict is all about. Spiritual warfare is centered on who the people of the world will give their allegiance to in worship. It is about who has control of the masses of people and who is vying for control of the world through the various nations.

You need to ask yourself, "What can I do to help bring about clear changes to the world that I live in?" Besides praying for your own personal needs, you need to be thinking about how you can find out God's will for the nations of this world and pray into the circumstances involving their existence and power. That is what can eventually affect us personally.

In this process of spiritual warfare with which we are involved, we must take heart and remember that God is in control of this world. He will say which authorities will be in existence and which ones will come to an end. His master plan will allow some nations to rise in power while others will wane and fall. He will determine what nations will have a godly positive effect on our lives and when they will fall as prey to evil.

Spiritual warfare is in existence today to fit into God's will and His way for the end times. All things of this world will come to a conclusion because God has a plan for a new heaven and a new earth that includes you and me.

There are many who do not even realize that there is such a thing as spiritual warfare. They continue with their lives thinking that life is only about how they live and how they can improve themselves without ever thinking that the world's chaos is a battle between the forces of God and the forces of the Devil. They think that life is simply a matter of choice, chance, or the survival of the fittest.

That is where you and I come in. We must take on this mantle of spiritual warfare in our prayer life and be part of the victory that belongs to God. Amen!

Chapter One: How Spiritual Warfare Began

IN THE BEGINNING GOD

Before we answer the questions surrounding spiritual warfare, there's another question about God that is intriguing. That question is, "What was God doing for all of eternity prior to the beginning of the good and evil that was released on all of His creation that started this whole process of spiritual warfare? And when did it begin?" Before He created man and woman to worship Him, what was God doing? Before He created the angels of the spiritual universe who eventually patrolled the physical universe, what was He doing to take up His time?

Of course, the answer is that with God Himself there is no time and there never was any need of time. He was not, and is not, limited by the constraints of a twenty-four hour day or a seven-day week. He only created time for the benefit of man. The difference between the element of time and the vastness of eternity is so far apart that we cannot even envision what God was doing. We can only imagine that God, who is self-sufficient, was complete within Himself. He needed no external assistance to feel needed or be fulfilled. He had extreme confidence in His own resources and power. We can only sense that within our limitations of time, the idea of eternity is far beyond our comprehension to understand God's perfect nature which allowed Him to be alone and simply be God.

Our God—whose understanding, the Bible reveals, encompasses both good and evil (Isaiah 45:7). He did not need time, but He created time in order to bring out His wonderful attributes in whom, and within what, He created. I'm sure that God knew the difference between good

11

and evil that was perfect in His own nature could potentially reveal a weakness in what He would create. God could only be a perfect God within the element of creation if what He created acclaimed Him to be so. That's why it was important that He create. The universe that He created displayed the best of His goodness, but it also revealed the propensity to do evil as well as the power to overcome that evil. God knew both the idea of good and evil, and His creation has shown both. That's the beginning and core of spiritual warfare. This idea of who God was before time began and His knowledge of both good and evil is what we must understand first before we enter the great battle that is being waged over the entire universe.

We know that God is a perfect God, despite the evil that is in this world. His nature of being perfect is revealed throughout Scripture. Everything about Him is perfect and all that He does is perfect. The Bible proclaims this through Moses and David:

> He is the Rock, His work is perfect; for all His ways are justice, a God of truth and without injustice; righteous and upright is He (Deuteronomy 32:4).

> As for God, His way is perfect; the word of the Lord is proven; He is a shield to all who trust in Him (Psalm 18:30).

Being perfect was also important for those who knew God and walked with Him. For Abraham, it meant that he was to emulate the perfection of God by walking before Him with integrity. In order for Abraham to be perfect, it meant that he was to be wholesome, truthful, and that he needed to adhere to moral and ethical principles. God said this to Abraham just when He was ready to reveal His everlasting covenant with him and with his son, Isaac. In Genesis 17:1 it says:

> And when Abram was ninety years old and nine, the Lord appeared to Abram, and said unto him, I am the Almighty God; walk before me, and be thou perfect (KJV).

Holding the same standard for God, in order for Him to be revealed as a perfect and a complete God, all sides of His nature needed to be disclosed. For example, after man fell into sin, in order for God to be seen as perfect in the minds and hearts of fallen man, He had to become man in order to redeem man. God's perfection is revealed in His plan of salvation. He had to become man in order to let men know that He understood the human condition and the sufferings of His created beings. This is clearly revealed by Him taking on the form of man through His Son, Jesus Christ, and tasting of the suffering which led to the death of Jesus. In Hebrews 2:10 it says:

> For it was fitting for Him, for whom are all things and by whom are all things, in bringing many sons to glory, *to make the captain of their salvation perfect through sufferings.*

THE CORE OF SPIRITUAL WARFARE

When it comes to spiritual warfare, many of us don't even know what the term really means from a Biblical perspective. We conjure up imaginary figures of angels and demons, fighting over things that are important to us. We pray and know that there is something going on in the heavens, but we are not sure what it is. We know that we are to gain the victory in this all mysterious sphere of influence, but many times we don't know how to do it.

Where does God fit into this picture? How much influence does He have in the power struggle of the heavens? Are there good angels versus bad angels? If there is such a struggle going on, does it really matter who wins? Do we have any influence in all of this in our prayer lives? This is what we propose to understand. This is the beginning of a calling that separates our spiritual life from the mundane chores and habits of our physical life.

This is where we enter into a realm that is so far out of the ordinary that if we could see the reality of it we would be scared beyond our wildest imagination. If we could only put on something like 3-D glasses in order to see how close the spiritual realm and its battles were, we would see that they are happening all around us and right before our eyes. If only we could see pictures of what it is like, just as if we were seeing it on television or in the movie theater. Good angels warring with evil angels for the rights of domination in a world created in its entirety for the glory of God.

We may carry on our daily living and struggles thinking that we have nothing to do with spiritual warfare, but Christian or non-Christian, all of us are seriously involved with the battle of good versus evil. We are part of that warfare whether we acknowledge it or not, or whether we want to be involved with it or not. Every day in which we do good things or others do evil things, we are involved. There is no exception. We are all a part of the masterminded creative force that either brings glory to God or an unwitting allegiance to the Devil.

The Christian is the gatekeeper of his soul; it is his soul that allows things in his life that can affect him and his family. The non-Christian is the gatekeeper of his soul and allows things into his life. Since the entire world is involved in spiritual warfare, both Christian and non-Christian can affect what transpires in all of our lives. The battles we may face, both spiritual and non-spiritual, affect all of us for good or for evil.

Christians and non-Christians are the gatekeepers of spiritual, political, or financial matters in every nation of the world and help determine the struggles that all of us have. This can be the influence of media information, job-related stability, relationships, laws, regulations, our spiritual relationship with God, or any other matter that can have an effect on the nations of the world. All in all, this leads us into a struggle whether we are a believer in God or a non-believer at work in the world.

The angels of the unseen world are gatekeepers as well, and can only be revealed through the opening of our spiritual eyes. The ungodly angels are part of a kingdom of a complex hierarchy of darkness and evil that seeks to bring deception and oppression on all of humankind. The godly angels of this spiritual force are for our care and protection and are clearly seen in the Old Testament in the example of the prophet

Elisha who asked God to reveal these protective angels to his own personal servant. The king of Syria who was warring against Israel had his war plans spiritually discerned by Elisha who then passed them on to the king of Israel. Once the king of Syria found out that Elisha knew his battle plans, he sent an army to surround Elisha in order to capture him. Elisha knew that the godly spiritual forces were surrounding him and that's when he asked God to reveal them to his servant who had expressed grave concern for their safety. We read this story in 2 Kings 6:16-17. It says:

> So he answered, "Do not fear, for those who are with us are more than those who are with them." And Elisha prayed, and said, "Lord, I pray, open his eyes that he may see." Then the Lord opened the eyes of the young man, and he saw. And behold, the mountain was full of horses and chariots of fire all around Elisha.

Understanding spiritual warfare should take us far above any concentration about our own personal life and into an understanding of God's mind and character in His unrelenting warfare with the Devil. We need to think about what God is thinking and what He is planning for the earth, not just about what He is thinking for our personal life and needs. His plans include the lives of others, our nation, the nations of the world, His plan for the world overall, the intergalactic control of the universe, and the defeat of the Devil in the end time.

There are many instances in the Bible when a struggle developed in which an angel fought with, or for, one of God's children. We can also see times when a godly angel stood on the side of good, and an evil angel stood on another side and represented that which was contrary to God and His will. The angels of the Lord acted often on behalf of God's people. They appeared, spoke, guided, guarded, and protected. Evil angels and demons acted on behalf of God's adversary, the Devil. This is the realm of spiritual warfare. The evil angels were polarized in their opposition to God and they fought against the godly angels.

Intergalactic Warfare

These good and evil angels stood with one group on one side of God and the other group on the other side of God. They were either for Him or against Him. This is the struggle between right and wrong, good and evil, truth and lies, unrighteousness and holiness. This is where you and I enter into the battle. This is the ultimate struggle for the good of life and for the will of God against the evil that seems to be supreme in this world.

A picture of this worldwide struggle is carried out in everything that man is involved in and in everything that he portrays. In the television industry or movie industry based in Hollywood, much of everything they produce centers on good versus evil. Murder, thievery, seduction, robbery, and war are all played out—for the most part in the context of good overcoming evil. Awards are given for the productions that show the best and the brightest in the movie industry.

In daily television and Internet news, pictures from around the world constantly remind us of the good conditions in the world that are appealing and the bad conditions in the world that are appalling. They refer to evil individuals who try to overtake the good in this world and how terrible and misguided that is. Reference is continually made to evil emperors or dictators who have been dealt with or need to be dealt with. Every day, good cops try to grapple with bad and aggravated situations in a good versus evil world. In the real world, the daily struggles that we see or encounter are a miniature view of the overall spiritual warfare and battle of life that is continually going on all around us. Clearly everyone sees and knows of this struggle.

This reminder of good against evil is a daily occurrence, a microcosm of the spiritual warfare between God and the Devil. The Bible clearly tells us that in the spirit world, we need to maintain a constant vigilance about spiritual warfare.

> This charge I commit unto thee, son Timothy, according to the prophecies which went before on thee, that thou by them mightest war *a good warfare*; holding faith, and a good conscience; which some having put away concerning faith have made shipwreck (1 Timothy 1:18-19 KJV).

16

In this passage, we are told that the warfare that we wage must keep us true to our faith so we can live with a good conscience toward God. We must fight against the Devil's tricks and lies, and not be deceived into returning to our former way of life as some did during the days of the apostle Paul. We must not return to sin, disgrace, and dishonor so as to make matters worse, as Paul also wrote about.

> Thou therefore endure hardness, as a good soldier of Jesus Christ. No man that warreth entangleth himself with the affairs of this life; that he may please him who hath chosen him to be a soldier (2 Timothy 2:3-4 KJV).

THE HUMAN FACTOR IN SPIRITUAL WARFARE

In the beginning of human creation, God placed the Tree of the Knowledge of Good and Evil in the garden of Eden in Genesis 2. Why did He do that? He knew about good and evil. His angels knew about good and evil. The Devil, or Satan, who is revealed as Lucifer in Isaiah 14 and Ezekiel 28 certainly knew about good and evil. Shouldn't God have kept the understanding of good and evil as far away as possible from Adam and Eve and His new creation, especially after Lucifer knew about good and evil and sin was birthed in his heart? Why would God want to take the chance that another part of His created world would fall into sin?

Yet He placed the one temptation that would cause the fall of man right in the middle of the garden of Eden! Yes, right in the middle of the garden, right in front of Adam and Eve. How preposterous is that? From a human standpoint, putting that tree right in the middle of the garden was senseless, absurd, and completely contrary to His godly nature. It's as if God wanted to test His own newly formed creation by first seeing if they would be obedient, second by putting them in the position to choose whom they would serve, and third, to be the determining factor in His spiritual struggle and warfare with the Devil. If they became disobedient, which they did, God wanted to see whether they would choose the good by serving Him or the evil by following the Devil. After the fall into sin through being tempted by the Devil, God wanted to give

His new creation the power of choice—to either serve Him or serve His new archenemy, the Devil. This choice was something different than the angels who had to make a onetime decision to follow after the Devil or remain faithful to their Creator, God. The struggle now moved to the human element in creation.

Of course, the Devil jumped at the opportunity to be the tempter. He told Eve the truth when he said that they would be like gods, knowing good and evil. Both Eve's and Adam's eyes were opened just as soon as they ate of the forbidden fruit. They now knew about good and evil just like the God who had created them. It was pure and simple rebellion and it was the Devil who lured them to his side and brought them right into the middle of the spiritual warfare that he had with God. He wanted this new creation on his side.

Satan also told Eve a lie by saying that she would not die. Truthfully, they were not like gods because that one act was an act of disobedience that brought them death. They were now a fallen creation with the knowledge of not only how to be good, but also how to be evil. They now knew what God knew and they had to be kept away from the Tree of Life. All of creation has been beset by a physical death sentence ever since their disobedience.

The Devil told Eve both the truth and a lie. The Devil is a master at that. That's what makes knowing the truth sometimes seemingly impossible. When Paul warned the church of Corinth about false apostles and deceitful workers appearing as apostles of Christ, he said that the Devil himself can be "transformed into an angel of light" (2 Corinthians 11:14 KJV). The Devil can present a distorted truth. There is always difficulty in discerning what the truth is when it seems as if a lie is presented as the truth. A lie can be as deceptively packaged as the truth so that it is hard to distinguish between what is truth and what is a lie.

Irenaeus, Bishop of Lyons, France, who lived in the second century church era and fought against the error of Gnosticism said, *"Error indeed is never set forth in its naked deformity lest being thus exposed it should at once be detected. It is craftily decked out in an attractive dress so as by its outward form to make it appear to the inexperienced, truer than truth itself."[1]*

The truth of God centers around the fact the He should be the object of our worship. With God being perfect, He needed created beings to be able to "worship Him in spirit and in truth" and to do the bidding of His will. He wanted to create not only angelic beings which He did; but after the fall of Lucifer, He wanted to create beings that would dwell on an earth that would have the physical and mental choice, or capacity, to either worship Him or ignore Him.

After the fall of the Devil, this choice was of paramount importance because of the rivalry of worship between him and God. God had the right to all of the worship of the universe, but the Devil wanted it. That is what made the Devil deceive Adam and Eve. That is the basic core of deception and spiritual warfare. He wants the worship that rightfully belongs to God.

With the advent of spiritual warfare between God and the Devil, the creation of the human factor of choice between right and wrong and good and evil is what I call God's *ultimate experiment*. It is a *testing of His principles* that would *showcase* some of His most outstanding attributes. This complicated warfare between these two most powerful of entities only brought about the enhancement of the greatest of God's character traits.

Bringing humans into the picture would satisfy God's sovereign wish to test the characteristics of obedience, holiness, righteousness, and godliness in His created beings. It would also reveal His attributes of mercy, love, grace, redemption, and forgiveness. All of God's children would have the wonderful benefits that could cause them to grow in the richness of their relationship with Him. Instead of God being only Elohim, the All-Powerful One, the one who had control and sway over all things, He became a God who exercised His attributes to meet the needs of His creation. We respond to His love, grace, and kindness; and

---

1. Irenaeus, *Against Heresies, Book One*, preface, public domain.

He is there for us now to meet our needs. Some of His divine relational names that show that He is there to meet all of our needs are:

- JEHOVAH-ROHI – The Lord my Shepherd
- JEHOVAH-RAPHA – The Lord our Healer
- JEHOVAH-JIREH – The Lord will provide
- JEHOVAH-SHALOM – The Lord is peace
- JEHOVAH-NISSI – The Lord our banner
- JEHOVAH-TSIDKENU – The Lord our righteousness

His created angels that had fallen were not the proper candidates for these attributes because they were spiritual beings that were too close to His own power and authority. As already stated, they had made their onetime decision to rebel against God. Angels don't die so it seems that they were on a different level than humans when it came to forgiveness and entering into a new realm as humans do after death. Also, they could not be a part of the determining factor as to who would win the battle of spiritual warfare because they were a part of it. Besides, as spiritual beings the evil angels helped to precipitate this new realm of spiritual warfare and they were not in the position to receive any of these loving attributes. The outcome of spiritual warfare could not be determined within the framework of the disobedient angels or the faithful angels. God needed a whole new creation to do this.

God would not be able to expend His attributes with anyone who would not have the power of choice to need them and also to receive them, so that He could use His energy to care for them. With the power of choice, His attributes would be implemented and relied on. God needed a new arena of creation with the option to either receive or reject these attributes. The fallen angels had already made their decision to rebel against Him and there was no longer a choice for them. He needed a new element—one that would have the ability to listen to His voice and either obey Him or disobey Him. I'm sure God knew all along that they would have to face His archenemy, the Devil. With this dichotomy in place, the warfare in the garden of Eden and on the human stage had begun.

The act of creation was an absolutely necessary decision after the Devil disobeyed God. The Devil was a spiritual being and failed as a dedicated and obedient servant of God. He was on a near par with God Himself, being created as close to God as he was and as perfect as he was. After his fall, the spiritual conflict between God and the Devil needed to be decided other than in the dominance of the spiritual conflict between these two that had already developed in the powers of heaven. The forces of the principalities, powers, and warfare in heaven were in place and the battleground would be the earth itself. The conflict between good and evil would find its place on a created earth, and we are part of the process of winning and losing. The particular battle lines that have been drawn between these two most powerful of enemies make *Star Wars* of movie fame dwarf in comparison.

As we worship God and fall in line to do battle against the work of the Devil, this creates more influence for God in the earth and less for the Devil. As we are obedient to God, we become less of slaves to the Devil and more of servants to God. Therefore, our part is to allow more influence on the earth for God and less for the Devil. This influences the battles in the heavens. That is when God takes over completely and the battle becomes His. His influence in our lives puts the Devil on the run because he no longer has any territory on this earth to do battle because we are worshiping God and are obedient to Him.

As an example, it was always God's presence in every situation that made all the difference in the world. It was His presence and power in battle against the Devil that would bring victory for His people. In the Old Testament when the children of Israel marched into battle, it didn't matter if their army was outnumbered. What mattered was that they had the presence of God with them in the form of the Ark of the Covenant. All they had to do was to worship God and be obedient to Him and the battle would be theirs. The battles that they fought weren't so much between them and their enemies because it was God's presence that would fight for them through spiritual warfare against the Devil for the territory they needed in establishing the power and strength of their nation. The priests carried the ark on their shoulders, but it was God who brought the victory. The battle became God's battle against the Devil, and God was always victorious when His people were obedient to Him.

Another example was when Joshua was fighting in his first major battle in which he was to take the city of Jericho. He encountered a mighty warrior that was standing near him with his sword drawn in his hand. Joshua didn't know who he was, but he wanted to know whose side he was on. It was similar to what President Abraham Lincoln said during the Civil War. Lincoln wasn't worried about God being on his side, he said, "it is my constant anxiety and prayer that I and this nation should be on the Lord's side."[2] We read the mighty warrior's reply to Joshua:

> And then this, while Joshua was there near Jericho: He looked up and saw right in front of him a man standing, holding his drawn sword. Joshua stepped up to him and said, "Whose side are you on—ours or our enemies'?"
>
> He said, "Neither. I'm commander of GOD's army. I've just arrived." Joshua fell, face to the ground, and worshiped. He asked, "What orders does my Master have for his servant?"
>
> GOD's army commander ordered Joshua, "Take your sandals off your feet. The place you are standing is holy." Joshua did it (Joshua 5:13-15 MSG).

Notice that the commander of God's army said that he was on neither side. That's because the real battle was not about the warfare on the ground between Joshua and the city of Jericho. This man was commanding God's army in the warfare that was going on in the heavens. True, Joshua's problem was between him and the enemy city that he was confronting and he was commanded by God to take it, but there was something higher at stake. The real battle and the commander's concern was the warfare that was taking place in the heavens. These powers of

---

2. Francis Bicknell Carpenter, Six Months at the White House, (Bedford, MA: Applewood Books, 1866), 282.

the heavens are not mentioned there in that Scripture, but truly God's commander was fighting against evil principalities and powers and he was there to inform Joshua what was happening. Of course, Joshua was involved in the earthly battle, but the most important thing for him despite what he was going through, was that he was standing on holy ground which meant that he needed to worship God in order for God to have the ultimate victory. This diminished the influence of the Devil in the earthly battle and increased the influence for God in what He wanted to do in the lives of the children of Israel. In spiritual warfare, this is what God needs in fighting the Devil.

Still another example was in that renowned battle of the armies of Israel against the Philistines in 1 Samuel—the one that involved David and Goliath. The battle really wasn't between those two great armies that were gathered together against each other although they were both there. This battle was God's battle, and David and Goliath were symbols of the vast struggle between the good and evil in the world. After David killed Goliath, Israel pursued the Philistines and plundered them as they ran for their lives. This battle was part of the great spiritual warfare between God and the Devil. David told Goliath:

> "You come to me with a sword, with a spear, and with a javelin. But I come to you in *the name of the Lord of hosts, the God of the armies of Israel, whom you have defied.* This day the LORD will deliver you into my hand, and I will strike you and take your head from you. And this day I will give the carcasses of the camp of the Philistines to the birds of the air and the wild beasts of the earth, that all the earth may know that there is a God in Israel. Then all this assembly shall know that the LORD does not save with sword and spear; *for the battle is the Lord's*, and He will give you into our hands" (1 Samuel 17:45-47).

These battles between God and the Devil were over who would receive the worship of creation. It was over who would have authority over the universe and over God's created beings. God had the corner on the market when it came to authority and worship, and Satan wanted to replace Him. The desire and craving for worship from the Creator of life was not about an egocentric powerful God who had gone amuck or who had a severe personality problem. Nor was God so self-centered that he desired misguided attention.

It was far greater and more universally shattering than that. At stake was which God would have the authority to bring his attributes to the created world. Would it be the Creator—the God of peace, mercy, love, and grace, or would it be the usurper god who created war, hatred, violence, deception, lies, and murder? The spiritual warfare between God and the Devil reveals the variance and horrible conflict between these two giants of the universe. In all of God's creation, who will be called upon to worship whom?

The creation of man and woman with this all-powerful human choice of who they would worship was absolutely necessary to help determine who would dominate the heavens. Who would be the choice of worship since the Devil tried to take it from God? Who would the new created beings worship—God or Satan? This is the crux of the warfare that started so simply in the garden of Eden, but now extends to created beings all around the globe and throughout the universe. Therefore, spiritual warfare is not between the Devil and me or the Devil and you, it is between God and the Devil! Period.

Yet, the difficult part of this entire scenario for us is that we are involved in this battle between God and the Devil, and it wasn't even our choice. We weren't selected by God to enter into a match like boxers who know the odds ahead of time when they are fighting in a ring, and who fight for their lives and reputation. For us, it was as if we were minding our own business and were mugged when we were walking down the street; we are fighting with an unseen warrior who's hiding in the shadows of darkness in a dimly lit alley.

It's God and the Devil who are fighting and they are fighting for control of the galactic universe. The spillage and overflow of their warfare runs over into us on earth. It has become a battle in which both God and the Devil are fighting for influence and control in our lives. It causes havoc and grief to us on a daily basis. God tries to get us to live for Him while the Devil attempts to interrupt our lives to do evil in any way that he can. We find ourselves born to help create the influence of these powers in the world that we live in as we struggle on our jobs, for our family, for health, wealth, and for blessings each day. That is why to whom we give our allegiance and live for is of the utmost importance.

God could have totally destroyed the Devil and the fallen angels immediately, but instead He left the day-to-day struggle and determination of this warfare and worship to His newly created beings. You and I are a part of this massive struggle that affects the total universe and all of eternity. Who we worship and serve is of extreme importance.

LUCIFER

In order to grasp spiritual warfare and how it pertains to us, the first angel that we need to expand our understanding of in this power struggle is the Devil, otherwise known as Lucifer. Lucifer was not God, but he was created by God. He was created by God with extraordinary powers and ability that placed him in importance right next to God and to His throne. In Ezekiel 28, we read that God had an issue with the evil leader of Tyre, a neighboring nation of Israel on the Mediterranean coast and a prominent power of the day. Suddenly, this prideful leader of Tyre seemed to have waned in importance as the text takes a turn and begins to speak about a great, powerful and perfect being of God's who was no longer perfect. It speaks of Lucifer who is also known as the Devil, Satan, the prince of the power of the air, the god of this world, an angel of light, the accuser of the brethren, among many other names that describe the things he does.

As a powerful type or foreshadowed symbol of evil leadership itself, the Devil became a representation of one who had been in Eden, the garden of God and who had become filled with sin. The Prophet Ezekiel spoke against this individual who was evil and filled with pride because of his beauty, and whose wisdom was corrupted because of his brightness. Lucifer is not named in the text, but the description is unmistakably Lucifer, or Satan, the Devil.

As far as Lucifer's perfection is concerned, this is what the Bible says about him in that passage:

> You were in Eden, the garden of God; every precious stone was your covering: the sardius, topaz, and diamond, beryl, onyx, and jasper, sapphire, turquoise, and emerald with gold. The workmanship of your timbrels and pipes was prepared for you on the day you were created. You were the *anointed cherub who covers*; I established you; you were on the holy mountain of God; you walked back and forth in the midst of fiery stones. You were *perfect* in your ways from the day you were created, *till iniquity was found in you.* ...Your heart was lifted up because of your beauty; you corrupted your wisdom for the sake of your splendor; I cast you to the ground, I laid you before kings, that they might gaze at you (Ezekiel 28:13-15, 17).

How was iniquity found in the heart of Lucifer? Where did sin come from? Did God create sin? Was God responsible for the evil that is such a big part of creation? We find out that God not only knew about evil, but the Bible says that He created evil, or calamity. God is the one who knows not only about the good things of life, but also the evil things. I am not speaking about dualism, the doctrine that there are two independent divine beings or eternal principles—one good and the other evil. I am talking about one God who knows the difference between good and evil, and who is the personification of good, period. Therefore evil and sin cannot be imputed in God as essential blemishes in His character and work, but it does say this quite clearly about our great God who is in control of all things:

> I form the light, and create darkness: I make peace, and *create evil*: I the Lord do all these things (Isaiah 45:7 KJV).

Lucifer was God's right hand angel. Who knows how long he was a perfect created being. He was in the garden of God and in the holy mountain of God from the beginning. He was the anointed angel of God who overshadowed, fenced in, protected, and screened in the entire universe of God. He was established by God and within God's holy mountain where God's throne was. He walked wherever he wished to walk. He was created so near to the heart of God that God called him perfect. He possessed the highest degree of skill, excellence, and quality. I believe he would have had knowledge of just about everything that God knew, including evil. He would have known the difference between good and evil, right and wrong, and God allowed Lucifer to have that understanding. Lucifer seemed to be the perfect embodiment of what was the closest being to God. He would have known the perfect way of good and the perfect way of evil. It was in this state of perfection and of the knowledge of good and evil that he birthed sin in his being in the form of rebellion.

With God knowing about sin and knowing the difference between good and evil, He did not sin nor did He care to indulge in sin. Who would God sin against? Neither did He rebel. Who would God have rebelled against? After all, sin is a rebellion against something or someone and there was no one higher or more powerful than God whom He could sin and rebel against. God was God, the Creator of all things, therefore He could not sin. Lucifer on the other hand, being created so close to God, and who knew the difference between good and evil, chose to do evil and rebel against God. Therefore sin was birthed in him and him alone. He had someone to sin and rebel against. The being he sinned and rebelled against was God.

In Genesis 3, he enticed Eve with what he himself knew. In Hebrews 8:1-6, we are made aware of the fact that certain aspects of the Old Testament tabernacle were patterned after things in heaven. More than likely, what is seen and known in heaven can be seen and known on earth. Therefore it would have been an easy thing for Satan to come out of the spiritual universe of the mountain of God and enter the physical universe of the garden of Eden and tempt Eve with the very thing that he was tempted with when he was in heaven.

Unfortunately, Lucifer fell from his perfect state and was cast out of God's presence. It was in this sinful, and now imperfect, state that Satan became the counterproductive created being who was opposed to

God. This is where spiritual warfare was birthed. In Ezekiel 28, Satan is depicted as a spinoff of the evil leader of the nation of Tyre. In Isaiah 14, it shows Satan mentioned as Lucifer in the context of the fall of the leader of the nation of Babylon. Isaiah not only shows Lucifer's pride, but how his role as the archenemy of God helped to weaken the nations. In these two passages about the Devil, it is clearly understood that spiritual warfare encompasses not just our own personal lives on a daily basis, but on a much higher level—who has control of the nations and of the world. This warfare among the nations is what impacts and changes the world and affects us. This warfare determines who is in control of the world and who is in charge. It says this about the Devil's attempts to overthrow the power of God:

> How you are fallen from heaven, O Lucifer, son of the morning! How you are cut down to the ground, you who weakened the nations! For you have said in your heart: "*I will* ascend into heaven, *I will* exalt my throne above the stars of God; *I will* also sit on the mount of the congregation on the farthest sides of the north; *I will* ascend above the heights of the clouds, *I will* be like the Most High." Yet you shall be brought down to Sheol, to the lowest depths of the Pit (Isaiah 14:12-15).

In this chapter we see the five "I wills" of Lucifer. He was determined in his rebellion against God. The Devil actually thought he could overthrow God. He believed that he could have removed God from His throne and replaced Him as the ultimate authority in the heavens. It was a plan that failed.

The Bible isn't clear as to who had jurisdiction over all of the angels before Lucifer fell into sin; perhaps Gabriel, Michael, and Lucifer were three archangels who helped rule all of the angels who were committed to their leadership. This is just speculation on my part, but my thought is that perhaps Gabriel had a third of the angels under his authority, Michael a third, and Lucifer a third. When Lucifer fell it was then easy for him to take the third of the angels with him who were under his command. These angels were deceived into rebellion with the Devil because of the leadership they were committed to. Revelation says about the Devil:

> And his tail drew the third part of the stars of Heaven,
> and did cast them to the earth (Revelation 12:4 KJV).

There are some who feel that the Devil believes that he can still overthrow God and His throne. I'm not sure about that, but one thing we do know is that in the future in the middle of the great tribulation, he seems to come to the conclusion that he either has to overthrow God or it's a lost cause. His plan is to deceive the world in the final grand battle of spiritual warfare during that time and take as many to hell with him as possible.

In that same twelfth chapter of Revelation, it says that Michael, the angel of God, will war with Satan and cast him out of the heavenly realm where spirits dwell. Satan fell from the throne room of God when he sinned originally, and then in Revelation 12, he and his angels will be cast to the earth out of that heavenly realm. Satan's role as the "prince of the power of the air" and the "god of this world" will come to a conclusion as he is cast to the earth for the final onslaught of his career against all humankind during the second half of the seven-year great tribulation. That's why the great tribulation is so filled with wrath. All of Satan's power in the final battle between him and God will be unleashed upon the earth. This will happen as the future of Satan is revealed to the world and he releases his devilish worst.

ANGELS OF THE HEAVENLY REALM

While humans are material beings and continue to struggle with desires in their bodies to either do good or follow their temptations to do evil, they are continually being tempted by the Devil and by his angels. The Devil's angels are not tempted because the evil desires leading to their fate are already sealed. Angels have a will and understand choice, and they made a one-time spiritual decision to serve God or not serve Him. Their position involving will and choice is somewhat different from our own. The angels of God are established in their holy and righteous state because they desired to do the will of God in a one-time decision to worship and please Him. Satan's angels are in a lost and sinful condition because they desired to rebel against God in a one-time decision to try and overthrow Him. Both good and evil angels cannot experience what we go through in terms of choosing between good and evil on a daily basis because God did not give them that power. Their decision was established in a one-time choice. The condition of both good and evil angels cannot be reversed.

The book of Revelation chapter twelve speaks about a great red dragon that is described later on in the chapter as the Devil. Verses one to five in this chapter is a historical section of this book of the future, as the Devil was poised to attack and kill what many believe to be Jesus at the time of His birth. We know that this fit in with Herod's plan at the time who was devilishly inspired to try and destroy Jesus because of his jealous rage after Jesus was born. As already pointed out, the fourth verse mentions the powerful influence that the Devil had on one third of the angels of heaven who also rebelled against God and fell with him.

Some of these angels have been bound and are waiting for their final judgment to be given to them by God. They are in a prison-like state while the rest of their counterparts have become part of a mass army of principalities, powers, rulers of the darkness of this world, and spiritual wickedness in high places. The angelic prisoners who are bound are described in 2 Peter 2:4:

> God spared not the angels that sinned, but cast them down to hell, and delivered them into chains of darkness, to be reserved unto judgment (KJV).

And Jude 6:

> And the angels which kept not their first estate, but left their own habitation, he hath reserved in everlasting chains under darkness unto the judgment of the great day.

The rest of the evil angels apparently are not bound and are referred to in the Bible as "angels," "demons," "devils," or "spirits." These are the ones who carry out all of the activity of the Devil, seeking to enter and control the lives of individuals. It does seem clear that while some evil angels are bound with chains, others are apparently temporarily bound or are free at certain times.

In Luke 8, Jesus met a demoniac of Gadara who had "devils for a long time." Out of the man, He cast a "spirit" whose name was "Legion" because many devils were in him. When Jesus went to cast them out, they did not want to go into the pit, an apparent reference to the bottomless pit where they would be bound, which they knew about. Jesus allowed them to enter into a herd of swine instead, and the swine fled down a steep incline and drowned in the sea.

In Revelation 9, reference is made of a horde of locusts that come out of the bottomless pit. These are apparently not really locusts because they do not damage the green foliage of the earth. They are hellish, supernatural, demonic beings that inflict horrible torment on men around the world for five months during the great tribulation. All of these evil beings that are free to roam the earth during that time are perhaps similar to those which we encounter in spiritual warfare day after day even now. The difference between now and then is that at that future time, the bottomless pit is opened for a massive display of their power during the great wrath that will be upon the earth. This is part of God's wrath and the warfare with the Devil and his legions that will inflict great punishment on the earth.

Before the fall of Lucifer, all of the angels had been created by God and for His glory. Even before the beginning of man when God created the angels as the first spiritual beings, the spiritual realm of the heavens was populated with them. Satan, who clearly existed before man, was created by God and so were all of the angels who, at that time, were all good angels. All of these angels were made just below God and above man. The book of Psalms indicates the placement of angels just above man.

> What is man that You are mindful of him, and the son of man that You visit him? For You have made him a little lower than the angels, and You have crowned him with glory and honor. You have made him to have dominion over the works of Your hands; You have put all things under his feet, all sheep and oxen—even the beasts of the field, the birds of the air, and the fish of the sea that pass through the paths of the seas (Psalms 8:4-8).

God's creation is vast and includes everything. He calls for all things to praise His name because of the fact that He created all things. In Psalm 148, it mentions the heavens, the sun, the moon, the stars, and the waters among many things. All of these things exist as a testament of praise to God. It also mentions angels, and that these angels were to praise Him because God created them. In speaking about all these things and the created angels, it says:

> Let them praise the name of the Lord, for He commanded and they were created. He also established them forever and ever; He made a decree which shall not pass away (Psalms 148:5-6).

We can see numerous times in both the Old and New Testaments where these created angels became involved in human encounters. These encounters involved both good angels and evil angels. Both of these types of angels have made an impact in the lives of individuals throughout biblical history. This is spiritual warfare at its greatest and highest, creating an influence that impacts the world and those who live in it. Some of these angelic encounters are clearly seen in the Bible.

When battling in the realm of principalities and powers, it is important that our lives are filled with the Spirit of God and not filled with anything else, or worse yet, empty! In Matthew 12, Jesus said that when an unclean spirit leaves a person it may try and return if it finds that the individual's life is empty and not filled with God. That evil spirit would bring seven other spirits to return with him to make that person's life more miserable than before.

This holds true not only for an individual, but also for a nation. The United States has done its best over the recent decades and much of the last half of the twentieth century to rid our nation of any reminder of our spiritual heritage. We have divested ourselves of any public display of religion in the public square and in schools where we teach future generations. Now the spiritual emphasis and the infilling of God's Spirit in our nation is gone. Our spiritual house has been emptied of any vestige of spiritual things. While there is a remnant who are willing to worship God "in spirit and truth" (John 4:24), much of the leadership of our nation has been torn away from the thoughts of the Declaration of Independence that declares our "firm reliance on the protection of divine Providence."

The Devil has had a field day in filling our nation with demonic trash and hedonism. Shame has come upon us because we have left our spiritual heritage. We have committed the sin that Esau committed. We have sold our spiritual heritage for a mess of pottage; and as a result, the Devil has been free to roam our nation at will.

Just like Eli's grandson, Ichabod, whose name meant "the glory is departed," all that is left for the United States is for someone to announce that God's glory is gone. During Eli's day the ark of God, symbolizing the presence of God, was stolen by an enemy's army. His sons were killed in battle, and Eli fell over backward and broke his neck and died when he heard the news. It was a calamitous day for Israel because the presence of God was now gone. It says this about Eli's daughter-in-law when she gave birth to a son at this time:

> Then she named the child Ichabod, saying, "The glory has departed from Israel!" because the ark of God had been captured and because of her father-in-law and her husband. And she said, "The glory has departed from Israel, for the ark of God has been captured" (1 Samuel 4:21-22).

We have come to a point in our nation that is similar to the one Apostle Paul found in Greece on his second missionary journey. While on Mars Hill in Athens, he found out that they were a very religious people, but didn't know who God was. The Greeks, who were supposed to be the intellectual people of that time, had come to the conclusion that any god and every god was the accepted god. He saw an inscription on their altar that read "to the unknown god." They had culturally come to the point of entertaining the thought that it was good to have some kind of god so they should have a place for any they did not know.

If we want to win the battle for our families and for our nation, it is a battle that will require all of us to fight a warfare that is more than just about ourselves and our own needs. As important as our personal battles are, the battle for our nation is critical. Without the nation remaining in a right relationship with God, our family strength will be eroded by a backslidden nation which has forgotten about God. God will have to deal with our nation and that will gravely impact our families.

The Bible gives clear warning that we have to call on God if our land is to be revived. It isn't good to give lip service to God. This is a fight in which the Devil wants our nation to fall deeper into sin and further from the will of God. However, it is not just the people who love and serve God who must call on Him; the political leaders who make the laws of the nation must call on God as well.

The message of repentance in the Bible was clearly marked for those who were religious people, but it was also for those who were political people. The message of repentance was designed for the humblest of people who served God in the Old Testament, and for the members of the church of the New Testament. It was also designed for the kings and political leaders of the land because they were confronted by God for their sins and for the fact that they were the ones who made the laws. Today, God needs our political leaders to help bring revival to our land. Concerning revival it says:

> O Lord, revive your work in the midst of the years! In the midst of the years make it known; in wrath remember mercy (Habakkuk 3:2).

> If My people who are called by My name will humble themselves, and pray and seek My face, and turn from

their wicked ways, then I will hear from heaven, and will
forgive their sin and heal their land (2 Chronicles 7:14).

In America, we are a very religious people, but we have refused
to take a stand for the true God in the public square. We have refused
to stand with those who founded our nation on Christian values and
principles. If there was ever a time that we needed to know who God
is and exalt Him publicly, it is now as our nation is vacillating between
many opinions about God. Our nation is approaching an historical period
of time when it is beginning to decline and collapse. This is spiritual
warfare—fought between God and the Devil in heaven, but echoed in
our hearts and lives on the earth. We are in this warfare and everything
is dependent on our worship of God or the lack thereof. We must ascribe
to Him all of the glory. We need God!

THE DESIGN OF THE "GREAT TRIBULATION"

The Bible mentions what is known as the great tribulation (Matthew
24:21 and Revelation 7:14). In Deuteronomy 4:27-31, we can clearly see
that the great tribulation was originally designed for the nation of Israel.
The church hadn't even been thought of except in the mind of God when
tribulation for Israel in the latter days was announced. Some translations
of the Bible call it distress, or trouble, or suffering. Nevertheless, Moses
clearly writes in that chapter that it shall be for Israel in the latter times.

In the future when the Christians will be taken from this earth when
the Lord meets the church in the air, Israel will need Michael, the guardian
angel of their nation. Revelation 12 says that Michael will cast the Devil
to the earth as the hatred that the Devil has against Israel will reach its
peak. This is part of the concluding intergalactic spiritual warfare of the
universe that affects the nations of the world and particularly the nation
of Israel. During the time of the great tribulation, the Devil will attempt
to strike a fatal blow against God's unconditional promise that He made
to Israel in the book of Genesis—and God will allow it.

That is why Satan has continually lured the nation of Israel into
disobedience over the centuries. The Devil has wanted to destroy Israel.

Intergalactic Warfare

The reason that Israel is targeted by the Devil is because they are the only nation with a biblical covenant with God. They are a chosen people with great spiritual blessings and promises that pertain to their nation and to all nations, and control over the nations is what spiritual warfare is all about. In Daniel, it makes it clear who the great tribulation is designed for, what will happen to the nation of Israel, and what the responsibility of Michael the archangel is.

> At that time Michael shall stand up, the great prince who *stands watch over the sons of your people*; and there shall be a time of trouble, such as never was since there was a nation, even to that time. And at that time your people shall be delivered, everyone who is found written in the book (Daniel 12:1).

Because he is still bitter about being thrown out of heaven, the Devil's tricks will be so evil during the great tribulation that he will place his full support behind a last ditch effort to fight against God, and against His Son, Jesus Christ. The final battle over the children of Israel will be right in the middle of that fight. If he doesn't know it already, the Devil will come to the conclusion that he cannot overthrow God, but he will do his best to turn as many individuals against God as possible during this time. He will fully support a last days man of sin called the Antichrist. The Devil is the one that will give power to this Antichrist. When describing the Devil as a dragon and the Antichrist as a beast, it says:

> So they worshiped the dragon who gave authority to the beast; and they worshiped the beast, saying, "Who is like the beast? Who is able to make war with him?" And he was given a mouth speaking great things and blasphemies, and he was given authority to continue for forty-two months. Then he opened his mouth in blasphemy against God, to blaspheme His name, His tabernacle, and those who dwell in heaven (Revelation 13:4-6).

The Devil gives impetus to the Antichrist to speak blasphemies. The Devil is the one who gives the impulse and the momentum to the

36

Antichrist to perform all of the evil deeds that he does. The Antichrist will be an exact copy of the evil of rebellion that the Devil first had when he fell into sin. Similar to what the Devil did in the beginning, the Antichrist is the one:

> Who opposes and exalts himself above all that is called God or that is worshiped, so that he sits as God in the temple of God, showing himself that he is God (2 Thessalonians 2:4).

Perpetrated by his evil deeds, the Devil will use everything at his disposal to wreak havoc on this world and cause as many people as he can to wallow in sin and destruction. He will do everything within his power to bring as much wrath, hatred, violence, and destruction as possible. He is cast to the earth during the middle of the great tribulation. That's why the second half of the great tribulation is so terrible. His entire power will no longer be concentrated in the air where principalities and powers rule. He will no longer cast a dark shadow over the ages as the "god of this world" and the "prince of the power of the air." His entire wrath will be cast out on the earth, and his angels will be with him. This is spiritual warfare at its most powerful peak and at its worst. In Revelation 12 it says:

> And I heard a loud voice saying in heaven, Now is come salvation, and strength, and the kingdom of our God, and the power of his Christ: for the accuser of our brethren is cast down, which accused them before our God day and night. And they overcame him by the blood of the Lamb, and by the word of their testimony; and they loved not their lives unto the death. Therefore rejoice, ye heavens, and ye that dwell in them. Woe to the inhabiters of the earth and of the sea! for the devil is come down unto you, having great wrath, because he knoweth that he hath but a short time (Revelation 12:10-12 KJV).

The wrath of God will also peak during the time of the great tribulation. The tribulation is a seven-year period, that is yet to be determined, on the children of Israel scheduled for sometime in the future (see Daniel 9:27). The first three and one-half years will be horrible, but the second three and a half years will be far worse.

In the book of Revelation, there are two different words used in the Greek for our English word "wrath." During the first half of the book of Revelation, which would be considered the first half of the tribulation, the word *orge* is used; it means a lighter, yet harsh form of the wrath, which is "anger, temper, agitation of the soul, impulse, indignation, or punishment."[3] For the most of the second half of Revelation, which would be considered the second half of the tribulation, the word *thümos* is used and means an even stronger form of the word wrath, which is "passion, heat, anger, and anger forthwith boiling up and soon subsiding again." It means "the wine of passion, inflaming wine (which either drives the drinker mad or kills him with its strength)."[4]

No one would want to portray God as drunk or madly infuriated, but this definition gives an indication of the mighty wrath that God will pour out, particularly in the second half of the tribulation. This is how the spiritual warfare that we are involved with today will move into the great tribulation full speed ahead. It will be a reckless and horrible time for the people of Israel and the world.

That is why we must preach the gospel to as many people as possible around the world in order to prepare them for the second coming of Christ and the great wrath that is coming upon the earth in the future. At that time, it will be an all-out assault on the Jewish people and the entire kingdom of heaven. The Bible does talk a lot about tribulation throughout history and says there has been a spirit of antichrist in the world since the time of Christ. Some feel that these tribulation days have been fulfilled throughout church history, but there will still come a future tribulation and a future Antichrist to try the world in the last days.

---

3. Thayer and Smith. Greek Lexicon entry for Orge, The KJV New Testament Greek Lexicon, accessed August 9, 2013, http://www.biblestudytools.com/lexicons/greek/kjv/orge.html.

4. Thayer and Smith. Greek Lexicon entry for Thumos, The KJV New Testament Greek Lexicon, accessed August 9, 2013, http://www.biblestudytools.com/lexicons/greek/kjv/thumos.html.

Chapter Two: Men of God and Spiritual Warfare

ABRAHAM

Abraham had warfare with some of the cruelest of principalities and powers that fought against godliness. During the days of Sodom and Gomorrah, these evil forces had turned the beautiful fulfillment of the sexual experience designed by God into the vilest and most wicked of all vices. What God meant as a microcosm of His creative work, the Devil turned into a twisted sexual ploy that had nothing to do with procreation. Homosexuality was a sinister and vile deviation from God's original plan of creation and man's involvement in procreation. How devastating this has been to God's holiness and righteousness. Years after the garden of Eden was lost for the human race, God had established a godly family in Abraham through whom He could work. God saw the actions of the Sodomites as a threat to His family plan and He was geared for action against them even before He destroyed them as seen in Genesis 18:

> And the Lord said, "Because the outcry against Sodom and Gomorrah is great, and because their sin is very grave, I will go down now and see whether they have done altogether according to the outcry against it that has come to Me; and if not, I will know" (Genesis 18:20-21).

Who were the ones who made this outcry against the cities of Sodom and Gomorrah? Did God Himself simply look down and observe the outcry of sin? Were the evil principalities and powers too obvious in their gloating over the city? Did the righteous angels of God have enough of the lifestyle of Sodom? Had they complained to God about this blatant sin? Were the righteous angels having a tug-of-war with the evil principalities of angels who were still trying to dominate the cities? Who knows? But in any case, it was God's warfare, not Abraham's.

The outcry had to be answered by God. The righteous principalities and powers were in place to bring judgment. Spiritual warfare was about to be tipped in favor of godliness. The destruction of Sodom and Gomorrah was on the horizon. Because Abraham talked with God, he knew what was about to happen. He asked for clemency through the mercy and forgiveness of God, in case there were enough righteous people there, but it was to no avail. God is always ready to grant forgiveness when repentance is offered up to God, but if not, judgment will follow. Abraham knew the city was about to be judged and destroyed.

God sent two godly angels to destroy these twin cities. No doubt these angels were warriors with vast experience. Abraham's nephew Lot was in the city of Sodom and about to fall to the same fate as all of the evildoers, but because of the pleading of Abraham, Lot was delivered. This spiritual warfare in this case was not centered on Abraham or his nephew, Lot; it was focused on the godly principalities and powers that won the day in this great clash of godliness against evil. Evil was destroyed in the cities of Sodom and Gomorrah!

Although this was spiritual warfare on a personal level because of Abraham's nephew, Lot, it was far greater than that because it reached untold numbers of people in the warfare over the cities of Sodom and Gomorrah then—and in centuries to come. Abraham pleaded with God to spare those cities if God could find a few righteous people there. The cities were not spared.

Just like Abraham, we too need to lift our eyes to greater and more important battles than our own personal ones. At stake are the various nations of the world and the level of influence the Devil has on their existence and their people. At stake too, is America, the great superpower that God has used time and time again as a godly influence, particularly in the area of missions. Our personal battles may be important to us, but God wants us to get involved with the spiritual warfare that affects the entire world. It is a tug-of-war between Himself and the Devil who is doing his best, or should I say his worst, to create as much havoc in the world as possible during these last days.

JACOB

Jacob had a powerful encounter with one of God's angels. He was a man who was intent on doing all that he could for God, even though he was sometimes terribly misguided. After alienating his brother Esau by stealing his birthright, he needed reaffirmation about the covenant that God made with Abraham and Isaac, his father and grandfather. He departed from his home with his parents, Isaac and Rebekah, to find a wife from his mother's family. Genesis 28 records that he had a dream of a ladder that reached to the heavens. On this ladder, he saw the Lord God on the top of it with angels, ascending and descending on the ladder. Jacob had a peek into the godly spirit world where angels lived and carried out the mission of God around the world.

Later on in Genesis 32, Jacob had to finally meet his brother Esau and settle old differences. He entered into the world of principalities and powers when he wrestled with what the Bible calls a man, but was more than likely an angel of God as mentioned in Hosea 12:4. This is one of the most beautiful, powerful, and striking encounters that visualizes warfare with an angel. Jacob's wrestling with this godly angel depicted the inner struggle that he had when it came to trusting God. His inner struggle showed his lack of confidence in what he was about to face. He wanted assurance from the angel that God was still with him. He held on to the angel all night until he convinced the angel that he needed God's blessing. He wrestled with him and demanded a blessing. With the struggle that he faced the angel told him that he had "power with God and with men, and hast prevailed" (Genesis 32:28 KJV). His struggle was so immense and intense that the angel changed his name from Jacob to Israel, from "deceiver" to "prince." Jacob received his blessing and knew that he had met God face-to-face.

Both of these experiences show a relationship with angels that Jacob had that were part of the spirit world. Jacob dreamed of the presence of God as he saw the angels of glory descending to him and ascending from him. It seemed as if he could almost reach out and touch them. He saw the beauty of the angels of glory. He was finally able to touch one of them as his next mighty experience drew him into actual combat with a mighty angel of God.

His ability to be with God and to stay with him teaches us that no matter what we are facing in this life, if we hold on to God, He will be there for us. Jacob's warfare shows us that we can stay with God in His presence and God will never leave us or forsake us, but will bless us and guide our lives. We too should not give up; we should wrestle with God until He answers our prayers as He will be there to meet all of our needs. His wrestling with God's representative speaks to us that yes, we are involved with a warfare that is heavenly and beyond the scope of our understanding or our imagination.

MOSES AND THE PASSOVER ANGEL

The Passover angel was another encounter with the forces of heaven that focused on the nation of Israel after Joseph, the son of Jacob, was sold as a slave and brought to Egypt. Joseph's entire family eventually came to Egypt because of famine where they lived, but their offspring became slaves. Four hundred years later in the book of Exodus, God sent Moses to deliver the children of Israel; and the angel of the Lord was sent to deliver God's people. This visitation was during the horrible killing of the firstborn of Egypt by a powerful being that the Bible calls "the destroyer." The children of Israel were instructed to slay a lamb for each household and apply the blood of the animal to the doorposts of their homes. When the Lord saw the homes of the children of Israel that were protected by the blood applied to the doorposts, the destroyer passed over them, hence the name "Passover," which is one of the great feasts of remembrance for Israel.

Spiritual warfare is not just a personal thing even though it may seem like it. It involves the nations of the world and how much the Devil has influence on them for evil. God is always meaning things for good in any nation while the Devil is fighting contrary to God's will and God's plans for godliness and righteousness. The deliverance from Egypt was not just for Moses; it was a spiritual encounter involving the principalities of God that brought about the beginning of the failure of a superpower, Egypt, and the birth of a new nation, Israel. God would fight for them. He told the children of Israel through Moses:

> And Moses said unto the people, Fear ye not, *stand still*, and see the salvation of the Lord, which he will shew to you to day: for the Egyptians whom ye have seen to day, ye shall see them again no more for ever (Exodus 14:13 KJV).

I often compare the slavery of the children of Israel in Egypt with the slavery of the Africans here in the United States. The deliverance of the children of Israel from slavery in Egypt caused a new and separate nation to be birthed—one that became one of the great nations in all of history. Through that great time of spiritual warfare, Israel became one of the enduring powers of all time, and even when they were extinguished as a nation, they remained a lasting people for God's glory, despite their disobedience and many losses.

In a similar way, the African-American people were delivered from slavery through the signing of the Thirteenth Amendment by President Abraham Lincoln in the nineteenth century. Instead of becoming a separate nation as Israel had, they remained in the United States to help America become a giant and enduring superpower. Without that victory over slavery during the Civil War, America would have split into two separate nations and would have never become the great nation that it became. Through the spiritual warfare of that time, as well as other circumstances, America became a great superpower. The Devil wanted to conquer and divide America, but America stayed together and helped bring about the rebirth of the nation of Israel in the next century as part of God's plan for the end times.

We have come to realize that it is God's Son, Jesus Christ, who sits above all of the principalities and powers, and He is in authority over the nations. God is in charge. God is in command. These other authorities—these principalities and powers—are on a level below the authority of God and His Son Jesus. The nations, its leaders, and the leaders of the evil principalities are subject to God. Therefore, our warfare comes under the jurisdiction of God and His Son. We need never to worry or fear the spiritual warfare that we encounter. God moves the nations of the world because they are in His command.

ELIJAH AND THE FALSE PROPHETS

There is something to be said about any spiritual battle similar to the one Elijah encountered with the false prophets of Baal in 1 Kings 18. Baal was a false god and an idol. Prophets who did not know the one true God put their reliance and financial attachment to this false god that could bring them notoriety, financial income, and stability.

During the days of the Prophet Elijah in the ninth century BC, the name "baal" could be applied to many gods of the Middle Eastern world. It could be used in reference not only to a false god but to humans, to creative forces such as thunder and lightning, and also as a false name for the true God. The name has an ancient etymological definition as "Lord." That's why there was so much confusion about God during this time and why this great battle between God and Baal was necessary.

By Elijah's day, there was a real competition between the understanding of who Baal was and who the true God was. This involved not only a distinction between the false prophets and the true prophets, but a distinction between opposing spiritual forces. This was not only a competition between false and true principalities and powers, this was an outright understanding as to who the true God would be. Who was really God? Was it Baal or was it the God of Israel? This transcended the spiritual forces of principalities, powers, rulers of darkness, and the spiritual wickedness of high places in the heavenly realm, and demanded an answer from God Himself.

This was an epitome of the classic struggle between the forces of good and evil. Although demonic forces are not specifically mentioned in this passage of Scripture, we know that it is a picture of what the power struggle of spiritual warfare entails. It was good versus evil, God versus the Devil. As the story goes, 450 prophets of Baal and 400 prophets of the grove were lined up with King Ahab of Israel. The prophets of the grove were supporters, and probably sympathizers, of the prophets of Baal. More than likely they were riding the fence when it came to the powerful influence that the prophets of Baal had over King Ahab and the people of Israel.

Ahab was the king of Israel at this time, and was in a long line of evil kings of Israel who had allowed idolatry to take hold in the northern kingdom of Israel. The Bible tells us in 1 Kings 16 that when King Ahab became king he did evil "more than all that were before him" and that along with his wife Jezebel, he "went and served Baal, and worshiped him" (1 Kings 16:30-31). Little wonder that the evil prophets of Baal and of the grove had so much control in the land. The evil forces of principalities and powers were prevailing in the lives of its political and spiritual leaders. They were winning the spiritual warfare battle. That's why evil can have so much influence. Leaders and people of any nation, who continually do evil and give in to evil principalities and powers of the air, will give no place for the godly powers of the heavens. Therefore godly beings will have no influence in the nation and the nation will collapse.

When the contest with Elijah and the God of heaven against the prophets of Baal and the evil principalities and powers was enjoined, they both had the opportunity to call fire down from heaven onto a prepared sacrifice. The prophets of Baal failed, even after they called on Baal all morning long. Elijah, on the other hand, was able to call down fire from heaven even after soaking the entire altar and sacrifice with water. God answered Elijah and proved that He was more powerful than Baal. The godly forces of principalities won over the ungodly forces of Baal to prove that the worship of God is central to the struggle of spiritual warfare.

Intergalactic Warfare

As mentioned in the previous chapter, God puts the responsibility of the success of any nation not only upon the religious leaders of the nation, but also on the political leaders. There is no doubt about it: political authorities have great influence in the nation they are serving. The people of any nation are greatly impacted by those who are ruling over them. Nations are punished not only because of the failure of their spiritual leaders, but because of the failure of their political leaders. That's what happened to the nation of Israel when its kings continued on a wayward path. God had to punish them. That's also what happened to wicked King Ahab and his wife Jezebel during this time.

On the other hand, a nation can be saved, as it was during the preaching of Jonah when the king of Assyria repented along with his people. That is why we need to take responsibility for our nation and pray for it and its leaders. Through prayer and intercession, we can be an overruling power in the spiritual realm of principalities and powers. It is in this realm that we need an intervention by God for the nations of the world. We need to understand God's master plan for the nations, who the ruling superpowers are, when they come to power, and when their power ends. We need to know how to "pray through" for these nations in order to know how God is directing them. We need to know God's will for the nations so we can do His bidding and pray for His will in the land. Our praying through to victory can birth the influence among leaders and among God's people to create a godly influence for each of the nations of the world.

This is why spiritual warfare in prayer for the individual, the family, the neighborhood, the state, and the nation that one is living in is so important. When our prayers rise above and enter into the realm of principalities and powers, we enter into the spiritual warfare of prayer for the nations. I call this intergalactic warfare. This includes prayer for the nation that one is living in, as well as prayer for all of the nations around the world and the universe that God rules and controls. This, in turn, impacts the gospel being preached around the world and how many people are converted to Christ.

David Siriano

JOB

The story of Job is another intriguing and compelling narrative of the struggle between good and evil. It is a "top gun" story of the greatest power for the good and the greatest power for evil. God and the Devil were debating the life of Job. You can't get any higher than God and the Devil in a power struggle of words and choices over a single life on the earth. God and the Devil are the two greatest powers in the Bible who have the single most major impact on the face of the earth. That is what this struggle was about.

One day when God had a conference with the powers of the universe so they could give account to Him, the Devil was among them. In a bragging declaration to the Devil as to the fortitude and will of Job, God asked the Devil if he had considered, or looked closely enough at, the life of Job. After all, Job was God's trophy of divine mercy and grace. He was God's prime candidate for the "Most Valuable Person in Life" award. Job was considered by God to be living as perfect of a life as humanly possible. He was a complete person, pious and gentle. He had no faults that were meaningful.

There was a massive power struggle between God and the Devil over who had the most influence over Job, and the Devil cited the fact that He didn't think God was playing fair. The Devil accused God of putting a hedge, or protective shield, around Job, his home, and all that he possessed. With complete confidence in Job that he would pass the highest degree of the principalities and powers test, God lifted that protection and allowed the Devil to have the power to touch all that he had—except Job himself.

The Devil did his dastardly worst in throwing the book of temptation and destruction at Job. He was allowed by God to take away all of his possessions, and even his children. Can you imagine that? God is in charge of life and death? Job, who was making sacrifices for the possible sins of his children, was apparently right. They may have been sinning and it cost them their lives. All of Job's children were killed as the house they were in fell on them by a great wind. His possessions were either stolen or destroyed by fire from heaven. Job did not curse God or blame Him nor did he emphasize his struggle with the Devil. He passed this first test in the fight of his life as the warfare between God and the Devil ensued.

This fight wasn't so much between Job and the Devil as it was spiritual warfare between God and the Devil, and poor Job was caught right in the middle of their fight. Sure, Job wanted to keep his possessions and his family, but this was a power struggle of a higher degree, more than Job's life, more than the lives of his children and more than what he possessed! You cannot get any higher in spiritual warfare than this, as evidenced as the pitiful saga of Job turned victorious through his outcry to God, his prayers, his dialogue with his friends, and the final intervention by God.

What we learn from the story of Job is that our spiritual warfare is really about the battle between God and the Devil over who will receive worship and praise! Even though the Devil hit Job directly with calamity, it was still not between Job and the Devil. The Devil wanted Job to curse God through the loss of his possessions and health, which would make the Devil victorious over God in Job's situation and would bring praise to the Devil by robbing God of Job's worship. He would have won an important phase of spiritual warfare.

Our struggle is just a minuscule part of that higher grand struggle. Of course, we have situations like Job such as financial problems, loss of business or job, health issues, and struggles over our children. There is no doubt that the Devil is very deceiving and tactical in his temptations. He is the accuser of any Christian who tries wholeheartedly to live for God. He tries to keep us in the same spiritual darkness that he so much enjoys. He attempts to keep us from discerning the truth. He entices us with the riches of this world. He brings fear into our lives and wants to harm us with physical infirmities, sicknesses, and addictions. All this happens because of his hatred toward the God we serve and our desire to worship Him only. Therefore the Devil is our enemy. The Bible calls him our adversary that seeks to devour us. However, God is there to protect us from the Devil and to give us life. Psalms 91 says:

> He who dwells in the secret place of the Most High shall abide under the shadow of the Almighty. I will say of the Lord, "He is my refuge and my fortress; My God, in Him I will trust" (Psalms 91:1-2).

And John 10 says:

> The thief does not come except to steal, and to kill, and to destroy. I have come that they may have life, and that they may have it more abundantly (John 10:10).

In Job's case, he took the high road and rested in the promises of God. His conclusion was not to fight against the Devil and blame him for his situation, nor name something and claim it as his own, nor try and change his situation mentally. Job could have felt that the struggle was between himself and the Devil, but he didn't. He accepted what he had to deal with. His friends told him that the reason for all of his losses was because he had sin in his life.

Some have cited Job 3:25-26 where it mentions Job's fear as reason to believe that Job lived in fear and in a state of dreadfulness. Actually just the opposite was true. Job 1 says that Job was "perfect" and that he feared, or reverenced God. He didn't fear horrible events happening in his life—he "shunned evil" (Job 1:1). I am sure that God, who bragged about Job to the Devil, would not have put him to the test to cause him such great sorrow and scorn if He thought that Job's faith was not perfect and that he couldn't handle it. The best Hebrew textual understanding was that that there was no reason that his fear and love for God had grown weak, and it was simply perplexing to him that such a complication of miseries had come upon him. The text supports the fact that once his problems began and he had no rest from them, then his troubles came continually. Job feared God and not his situation; it was the dread and awe of God that he lived in and respected.

It's so easy to put the blame on our human condition because sometimes we don't know what to do and we don't have all the answers during a time of trouble. In the gospel of John, in the case of the man born blind from birth, the disciples attempted the "name and blame game" and wanted to know who was the cause of his blindness—him or his parents. Jesus said "neither" and the answer that Jesus gave was a revelation of a higher good that the disciples did not see. Jesus stated quite clearly and distinctly in John 9:3: "Neither this man nor his parents sinned, but that the works of God should be revealed in him."

Our so-called friends today don't understand what God wants to reveal through us because of our trouble or losses. When something calamitous like that threatens our physical life and well-being, these friends say "you have sin in your life" or "you don't have enough faith." Of course, Jesus was outspoken when it came to making sure that sins were forgiven and he was critical of his followers with "little faith." But we can read where He had good reason for bringing that out in people's lives when necessary.

Some critics, however, are simply spiritually immoral when they use their extreme faith answers against others whose lives are involved with a broader spiritual warfare because of the events they are going through in their lives. They fail to recognize the higher struggle that is going on with the principalities and powers in the heavens over something that they know nothing about. They bring shame to the healing process in other people's lives.

During the next meeting that God had with the powers of the universe in the book of Job, God had one complaint for the Devil. Because of the Devil's accusations against Job while God was showing him off as His trophy during their previous meeting, the Bible says that at the Devil's request, God moved against Job to bring ruin to him without a good reason. God told the Devil:

> Have you considered My servant Job, that there is none like him on the earth, a blameless and upright man, one who fears God and shuns evil? And still he holds fast to his integrity, although you incited Me against him, to destroy him without cause (Job 2:3).

If it seems that sometimes our spiritual warfare doesn't make any sense and that life is not fair, that's the time to keep our absolute faith in God, because there could be a powerful struggle going on that has higher and greater implications than what we can see. According to the biblical story line, God was the one who made the ultimate decisions in the testing of Job. This shows us that through the entire story of Job, God was in control and not the Devil. That's a wonderful promise to all of us: that during the power struggle that we have with principalities and powers over issues here on earth, the Devil cannot do anything against us without God's permission and will.

The Devil then requested to harm Job with a serious illness and God gave him permission to do that as well, but he was not allowed to take Job's life. I love it! God is in control over issues involving our health and over the length of our days here on earth as well. The Devil afflicted Job with boils all over his body. Job's second test was to see how much he could physically endure without cursing God. God allowed the Devil to physically harm Job. The result was that Job did not curse God, so he passed that test as well.

People of misguided faith fail to realize that the horrible things we pass through may not only be inflicted by the Devil, but may have a design and connection with God Himself as a test of our relationship with Him. In our struggles over finances and over health and family issues, we tend to declare these as unacceptable in our walk with God, and as being only from the Devil, when, in fact, they could be allowed by God to actually increase or test our faith. Some people even go as far as to deny that anything bad could ever happen to us. We however must conclude that bad things can happen to good people and good things can happen to bad people. Justice and injustice can fall on both the good and the bad, no matter their relationship with God.

> That ye may be the children of your Father which is in heaven: for he maketh his sun to rise on the evil and on the good, and sendeth rain on the just and on the unjust (Matthew 5:45).

Intergalactic Warfare

The power struggle that unfolded between Job and his wife, and Job and his three supposed friends is a typical display of a worldly physical struggle that is under the heavy influence of the principalities and powers of the heavens. The struggle that unfolded between God and the Devil trickled down to the influences that these principalities and powers had over each individual's life—Job's wife and his three friends. The complete story of Job ends with him being victorious over these principalities and powers that used his friends to accuse him of sin and failure.

Job admitted that he was a sinner; in the end, his own sin was that he was still ignorant of God's total power to control the universe and the world in which he lived, even after the powerful answers he had given to his friends about God. He attempted to justify himself and his own struggle without a full understanding of God and His great power. God had to speak to Job; this caused him to repent and humble himself over his lack of understanding of what he was going through. All of this meant that God had power to control even the minute details of Job's life. In spite of Job's confession, God still called Job right and his three friends wrong because of their accusatory condemnation of Job. In Job 42 it says clearly:

> And it was so, that after the Lord had spoken these words unto Job, the Lord said to Eliphaz the Temanite, *My wrath is kindled against thee, and against thy two friends*: for ye have not spoken of me the thing that is right, as my servant Job hath. Therefore take unto you now seven bullocks and seven rams, and go to my servant Job, and offer up for yourselves a burnt offering; and *my servant Job shall pray for you*: for *him will I accept*: lest I deal with you after your folly, in that ye have not spoken of me the thing which is right, like my servant Job (Job 42:7-8 KJV).

Job had battled with the principalities and powers of the world and won! Job had to realize the awesome, sovereign power of God. God spoke to Job with great detail and explained that He had created everything, and that He was in charge of all life, which, of course, meant Job's life as well. In essence, God was defending His right to allow all these bad things to happen to Job when He practically gave the Devil unlimited access to Job and what Job possessed. Job trusted in God, but still lost everything. The happy ending to this story is that God reinstated him double of all the possessions that he had before, and he had seven more sons and three more daughters as well.

Some final thoughts at this point encourage us to make sure that our attitude is correct in regard to things that we must endure. In our inept attempt to prove our faith, we sometimes become like Job's three friends. We totally miss a patient and rewarding relationship with a loving God who has confidence that we will be victorious through any struggle that we may go through. We have a tendency to rebuke anything and everything in sight, and oppose anything that comes our way when we deem it out of our comfort zone and out of balance in our lives.

Sometimes we don't like what is happening to us or think that it's wrong for us so we rebuke the Devil and attempt to denounce things that may not need denouncing. We speak against anything that we determine is against the will of God, and sometimes we get it wrong. Many times we have imposed our will rather than trying to understand God's will, and sometimes we end up fighting against God and what His will is for our lives.

Of course, there are times when rebuke is necessary and we know that Jesus and the apostles battled against the Devil and demonic spirits as they took authority over them. We fight against these same evil authorities as well, so that they will have no part in our lives. But we must make sure that we are operating under God's authority for every given occasion with the power of the Holy Spirit in us, and not operating with our own will and mind-set.

Something disturbing like this happened on the apostle Paul's third missionary journey while he was at Ephesus. He had a very successful ministry for over two years that touched people all over Asia; as many people who heard the gospel came to Christ. There were miracles of healing and he was also casting out evil spirits that tormented people.

Apparently there were some who tried to copycat him in their own power. The seven sons of Sceva had the misfortune of trying what the apostle Paul did, and they met demons that turned on them and harmed them. It says in Acts 19:13-16:

> Then some of the itinerant Jewish exorcists took it upon themselves to call the name of the Lord Jesus over those who had evil spirits, saying, "We exorcise you by the Jesus whom Paul preaches." Also there were seven sons of Sceva, a Jewish chief priest, who did so.
>
> And the evil spirit answered and said, *"Jesus I know, and Paul I know; but who are you?"*
>
> Then the man in whom the evil spirit was leaped on them, overpowered them, and prevailed against them, so that they fled out of that house naked and wounded.

These men were part of a traveling group that practiced exorcism. In the Greek language, their father's name *Sceva* meant "mind reader."[5] No doubt these sons learned this practice from their father, using their mind or intellect to use deceptive practices to make it look like the exorcism they were attempting was a spiritual thing. In our ministry today, we must make sure that we in no way attempt anything like this. We must not just say whatever comes into our mind. We must not enter the realm of spiritual warfare and fight against spirits when we have no power over them, nor should we deceive people in our ministry. We must beware!

> But we have renounced the hidden things of shame, not walking in craftiness nor handling the word of God deceitfully, but by manifestation of the truth *commending ourselves to every man's conscience in the sight of God* (2 Corinthians 4:2).

---

5. Thayer and Smith. Greek Lexicon entry for Skeuas, The KJV New Testament Greek Lexicon, accessed August 9, 2013, http://www.biblestudytools.com/lexicons/greek/kjv/skeuas.html.

We in the Spirit-led community sometimes seem to follow every wind of doctrine instead of truthfully following the Spirit and mind of God. Many times we say that we are led by the Spirit of God, when in fact we are following our own spirit, our own feeling or motives. That's when we are misled and may mislead others. The mistake we make is, instead of listening to God's Holy Spirit (Spirit with a big "S"), we are in tune with our own spirit (spirit with a little "s") and perhaps another person's spirit. We let our own thoughts and motives get in the way instead of seeking God's will. We need to take note and submit our thoughts, ideas, doctrine, and ministry to others that can help us to be responsible, legitimate, and truthful servants of God. Nothing in us must be a sham or questionable; we cannot be acting in any way that may harm others or bring dishonor to God. We must make sure that we are truly following the Holy Spirit.

We freely toss out the phrase, "I rebuke you in the name of Jesus." That may be all well and good in certain situations, but we better make sure we are living totally under the authority of Christ in obedience to His will and have God's Holy Ghost power to speak that statement. We don't want to take the chance of speaking for God when He never directed us to speak for Him. In Jeremiah's day, that is exactly what happened to the many false prophets of his day. They said they were speaking for God when God said that they weren't. It says:

> And the Lord said to me, "The prophets prophesy lies in My name. I have not sent them, commanded them, nor spoken to them; they prophesy to you a false vision, divination, a worthless thing, and the deceit of their heart" (Jeremiah 14:14).

> I have not sent these prophets, yet they ran. I have not spoken to them, yet they prophesied. But if they had stood in My counsel, and had caused My people to hear My words, then they would have turned them from their evil way and from the evil of their doings (Jeremiah 23:21-22).

Intergalactic Warfare

There are two instances in the Bible that were phrased slightly different than the phrase "I rebuke you." In Zechariah 3 when Joshua, the High Priest, was standing to perform the work of the Lord, the Devil was there to resist him. It says that the Lord Himself rose up against Satan and said, "The Lord rebuke thee, O Satan; even the Lord that hath chosen Jerusalem rebuke thee" (Zechariah 3:2 KJV). The other instance is in the book of Jude when after Moses died, Michael the archangel was contending with the Devil over his body and dared not bring any accusation against the Devil but simply said, "The Lord rebuke thee" (Jude 9 KJV). We should hope and pray for the same wisdom so that God can use us in spiritual warfare in a proficient and accurate manner, operating with the knowledge and understanding of His will.

PAUL

Some would say, "Well, Job's story is from the Old Testament and things changed after Christ died on the Cross. We no longer have to live through the same things that Job did. We now have the right to claim continual and perfect health and every great and victorious situation in life." Well, not so with the apostle Paul in 2 Corinthians 12. He too had the Devil attack him both bodily and spiritually—just like Job. It was a spiritual battle, but he also had a health problem, which was a physical battle.

I am a believer in faith, healing, miracles, and that God answers our prayers, and that we should never give up on our quest for God to hear and answer us. However, just like Job, Paul had to endure something physical that was allowed by God. There are some people who because of their twisted belief in healing would say that Paul never had a health problem. They would rather believe that it was only a spiritual battle that he couldn't overcome. They would rather believe that it was some adverse spiritually controlled torment he endured instead of admitting it was also a physical sickness allowed by God. To be sure, the Bible says that Satan buffeted him, meaning that he was struck and mistreated with violence, which was spiritual, but it was "a thorn in the flesh."

We don't know what his infirmities were, but some don't want to admit that Paul would have had to live in continual pain or sickness. They wouldn't agree that it could be God's will if that happened to anyone. Their encouragement or lack thereof would be similar to Job's three friends. They would say Paul's problem had nothing to do with the physical. But they are wrong. The Greek interpretation supports the fact that it was both a physical and a spiritual battle. Anytime you are dealing with physical problems in your life, more than likely it involves a spiritual battle as well. Paul had to come to the conclusion that he would not be healed.

God said, "my grace is sufficient for you" (2 Corinthians 12:9). Paul had to surrender to the Spirit of God, and that God's grace would be sufficient for him to help him through something that he could not change. Can you imagine that God would say to Paul, "No, I am not going to deliver you of your spiritual oppression," if it was only a spiritual battle? How absurd is that? Paul did not receive a spiritual affliction to prevent him from being lifted up in pride because of his spiritual revelations. That would be counterproductive. It wouldn't make sense. Paul was carried into the "third heaven" where he had been given "abundant revelations," so he received a *physical* affliction to prevent him from being lifted up in any spiritual pride in the flesh.

Two things should be remembered here. 1) The difficulties and storms that come into our lives are not because we are doing something wrong, but because we are doing something good. 2) The truth of God's love and protection for us is not that He wants bad things to happen to us, but that He wants us to know that He will be with us when they do.

Paul was reminded that he was human and that he should not boast. His attitude would determine whether or not he would have victory in spiritual warfare and whether or not he could send the Devil fleeing from him. Paul's warfare was not to gain victory; his warfare was in victory. His battle was already won! His attitude determined that, and more than likely became, "Devil, get thee behind me; it is God who has asked me to endure this physical ailment. God has already won and I have victory!" Most definitely Paul had to fight a spiritual battle in this, but the spirit he was fighting was over his physical health. In his case, it was more important for him to win the spiritual battle than the physical battle of good health.

I have seen great faith in the lives of great people who trusted explicitly in our great God, yet they were not healed. Their victory in spiritual warfare was only completed in heaven once they arrived there. Healing isn't our goal only on earth; it is our goal to reach heaven where God is and be completely, totally, and spiritually healed once we see Christ!

Some Christians die because of natural causes; some die with grave illnesses, while others die accidently. All of us have known of Christians who have died in car accidents, plane crashes, or in catastrophic events of nature. Did that mean that their faith was weak or that it failed them? No! None of us knows the day that God will call us home, nor do we know by what circumstance. The bottom line is that sometimes it doesn't matter how we get to heaven—as horrible as that transition may be, the important thing is whether or not we make it there. That's the most important thing.

In Paul's case, he was given this thorn in the flesh imposed by a messenger of Satan to torment him. This was both a physical and a spiritual attack on the apostle Paul. It became a test of spiritual warfare in his life. More important than understanding what the thorn in the flesh and the messenger of Satan was is the fact that Paul was asked to endure with grace what God was putting him through. He rose above the realm of spiritual warfare and understood the valuable lesson that God was trying to teach him. His difficulty in the flesh contributed to the strength and perfection of his ministry. It was just like the suffering that Jesus went through that perfected Him. In this story of Paul, God spoke these words to him:

> And He said to me, "My grace is sufficient for you, for My strength is made perfect in weakness." Therefore most gladly I will rather boast in my infirmities, that the power of Christ may rest upon me. Therefore I take pleasure in infirmities, in reproaches, in needs, in persecutions, in distresses, for Christ's sake. For when I am weak, then I am strong (2 Corinthians 12:9-10).

DANIEL

In Daniel, we see graphic pictures of the great struggle of principalities and powers for influence and control over the nations. We receive a sense of the spiritual warfare in the heavens that dramatically affects what is happening on the earth. We can read about the end times and the Antichrist who will appear in the great tribulation. It is in Daniel 8 and 11 that we can see quite clearly what his evil deeds and personality are all about.

In the eighth chapter, we see a description of the struggle between Persia and Greece, two of the great superpowers of the time, which involved spiritual warfare in the lives of the children of Israel. After a dialogue of the power struggle between these two great powers, we read a description of how someone would rise to be an evil leader during the days of the nation of Greece. This person, known as Antiochus IV Epiphanes, would bring confusion and violence by interrupting the sacrifices of God's people in Israel during that time. He sacrificed a pig on the altar of the temple in Jerusalem as he raided Israel and brought destruction and murder to the land. He became an embodiment of evil for the last days of Israel after the kingdom of Greece would cease as a superpower. He became a type of the Antichrist himself who would arise in the time of the great tribulation.

In Daniel 11, we read further information about the spiritual warfare between two great powers that arise as an outgrowth from the power of Greece: Syria in the north and Egypt in the south. In this chapter after a long dialogue about their struggle over many years, there is another description of the Antichrist. These two chapters in Daniel end with descriptions of the horrible power that this man of sin will possess. The picture of the Antichrist is described in Daniel 8 and Daniel 11.

> And in the latter time of their kingdom, when the transgressors have reached their fullness, a king shall arise, having fierce features, who understands sinister schemes. His power shall be mighty, but not by his own power; he shall destroy fearfully, and shall prosper and

thrive; he shall destroy the mighty, and also the holy people. Through his cunning he shall cause deceit to prosper under his rule; and he shall exalt himself in his heart. He shall destroy many in their prosperity. He shall even rise against the Prince of princes; but he shall be broken without human means (Daniel 8:23-25).

Then the king shall do according to his own will: he shall exalt and magnify himself above every god, shall speak blasphemies against the God of gods, and shall prosper till the wrath has been accomplished; for what has been determined shall be done. He shall regard neither the God of his fathers nor the desire of women, nor regard any god; for he shall exalt himself above them all. But in their place he shall honor a god of fortresses; and a god which his fathers did not know he shall honor with gold and silver, with precious stones and pleasant things. Thus he shall act against the strongest fortresses with a foreign god, which he shall acknowledge, and advance its glory; and he shall cause them to rule over many, and divide the land for gain (Daniel 11:36-39).

In Daniel's attempt to understand the condition and welfare of the future of his people who were in captivity, he inquired of God for answers. In Daniel 9, Daniel was reading words of the prophet Jeremiah, trying to determine the years of the captivity of Israel. The children of Israel had been carried out of their land into captivity to the nation of Babylon, and Daniel had expectations that the people of Israel would return to their homeland sometime in the future. He was beginning to ask of God the things that affected the principalities and powers of the heavens.

What Daniel did in that chapter was to pray for his nation that was still in captivity. The nation of Israel had been taken captive by the Babylonians seventy years earlier and the people were five hundred miles from their homeland. He was clinging to the prophet's prediction that Israel was to return to their land in Palestine. In a state of spiritual warfare for the nation of Israel, Daniel rose above his personal battles with his enemies that we read about in the previous chapters. He interceded for his people Israel and asked God for forgiveness for his nation's sins, praying that God's anger would turn away from Jerusalem. The warfare that he was encountering was God's warfare with the Devil over the control of the nations and the control of God's people, Israel. Similar to the prayer of Nehemiah that he prayed on the return to Jerusalem from captivity when he took on the sins of the nation before God, Daniel's prayer reveals that he too took on the sins of the nation as if they were his own personal sins. His prayer included the following segments which we can also use in prayer for America:

1. He acknowledged God's covenant (verse 4).

2. He confessed the nation's sin, iniquity, wickedness, and rebellion (verse 5). (He seemed to speak of the sins of Israel as if they were his own sins.)

3. He realized that they had not listened to God's servants, the prophets (verse 6).

4. He acknowledged their unfaithfulness because of sin (verse 7).

5. He confessed the shame of their faces (verses 7-8).

6. He acknowledged the nation's disobedience to God's law (verses 10-11).

7. He realized God's curse and God's disaster was upon the nation, and that it was just (verses 11-12).

8. He knew that even though they had had disasters fall on them, they still did not pray as they should (verse 13).

9. He knew the nation had not turned from their iniquity in order to understand the truth (verse 13).

He understood in reading Jeremiah that Israel's time of Diaspora in Babylon would be for seventy years. This is when God revealed what is called in Daniel 9 as a seventy-week timeline for the nation of Israel based on the seventy-year period of their captivity. In Old Testament

Hebrew, the word "week" in this chapter is defined as "seven."[6] In context, with Daniel's mind on the seventy years of captivity, each week is not defined as a literal seven-day week, but as a seven-year period of time, with each day representing a year. Therefore, seventy "sevens" or seventy times seven amounted to 490 years. The angel Gabriel was dispatched to help Daniel know that a 490-year period of time was to unfold in stages, leading up to the end of time for Israel and the world. 483 of those years happened from the return of the children of Israel back to Palestine during Daniel's day until the crucifixion of Christ.

Then came the church age in which we are living now, so that the Gentiles could be reached for God in accordance with Old Testament prophecy. After that comes the final seven-year period that Daniel mentions in Daniel 9:27. The total 490-year period would climax with this seven years of trouble defined as the great tribulation. End time imagery of this climax is seen in numerous passages here. For instance, in Daniel 7, we read statements like these referring to the end times:

> The judgment was set, and the books were opened (Daniel 7:10 KJV).

> Behold, one like the Son of man came with the clouds of heaven, and came to the Ancient of days, and they brought him near before him. And there was given him dominion, and glory, and a kingdom, that all people, nations, and languages, should serve him: his dominion is an everlasting dominion, which shall not pass away, and his kingdom that which shall not be destroyed (Daniel 7:13-14 KJV).

> The Ancient of days came, and judgment was given to the saints of the most High; and the time came that the saints possessed the kingdom (Daniel 7:22 KJV).

---

6. Brown, Driver, Briggs and Gesenius, Hebrew Lexicon entry for Shabuwa`, The KJV Old Testament Hebrew Lexicon, accessed August 9, 2013, http://www.biblestudytools.com/lexicons/hebrew/kjv/shabuwa.html.

DANIEL'S INTERGALACTIC WARFARE

When it comes to spiritual warfare between nations and the changing of the guard of superpower nations within the framework of principalities and powers, no clearer picture can be seen in the Bible than that in Daniel 10. Just as he was in Daniel 9, he was fighting for the spiritual rebirth of the nation of Israel after the seventy years of captivity in Babylon. Here, he was caught up in a superpower spiritual battle in the heavens before Greece emerged in power. It was between the two great superpowers of Babylon and Persia which had dramatic effects on the nation of Israel.

Daniel 10 gives us a graphic picture of the workings of principalities and powers. This is one of the entry points to spiritual warfare; when it comes to the power struggle of the nations and the universe, it is what I call intergalactic warfare. In the confines of captivity, a revelation of truth had been shown to Daniel. He understood it as best he could and determined that it was something from God. He knew it was to happen at a later time, but he had confidence in its completion.

After this revelation, Daniel began to pray. He was in a state of prayer for three full weeks with no answer. He fasted during the entire time. Then a man came to visit him to further explain the revelation he had just received. This man was no mere mortal man. According to his description, he was sent by God from heaven. Some picture this as a possible Christophany, a visit by Christ, but more than likely it was a powerful angel sent by God. Either way, he was a powerful spiritual messenger who was deeply and seriously involved with spiritual warfare to the highest degree. He was in the middle of warfare of international proportions. What Daniel got involved with in his prayers was the passing of the superpower baton from Babylon to Persia. Babylon was going out as a superpower, and Persia was coming in as a superpower.

Daniel saw this spiritual messenger in a vision and it sapped his strength. As he saw the vision of this powerful individual, it caused Daniel to lie prostrate on the ground. The messenger touched Daniel and caused him to sit up upon the palms of his hands and knees. He was then commanded to stand up erect. The experience of being in the presence of this spiritual individual was so intense that Daniel could only respond with great fear and trembling. This is how powerful these angels are, and this is the warfare God has asked us to enter into as well.

The spiritual warfare in life's situations and difficulties that impact us connects us to the spiritual warfare in the realm in which God wants to reveal things of greater importance. We can become involved in things that are much larger than we could ever know or imagine. The problem is that we concentrate so much on our own personal things that we fail to understand the battles that are waged in the heavenly sphere. These battles are over control of powerful nations and over much of what happens right here on earth, literally around the world.

If we would fully understand what spiritual warfare is all about, we would realize that we are fighting over which principalities and powers will gain control of the church worldwide. We are also fighting for who has control over the nations of the world. We are fighting over which spiritual forces have the greatest impact over each nation and which leaders will lead the nations—whether good leaders will rule or bad leaders will rule. We are also waging warfare over the gospel being preached in all nations, praying for laborers to enter the harvest field, and praying for souls to be saved.

We must focus on the larger picture when we are praying. When we pray for our loved ones to be saved, we must realize we are on the spiritual edge of entering into prayer for souls to be saved around the world. When we pray for the church we attend and the people we know, we can easily enter into prayer for the church around the world, both the free and the persecuted church. When we pray for leaders in America, it's an easy step to expand that and pray for political leaders around the world. When we pray for our personal needs to be met, we can pray for people all over the world who may be struggling financially or who may be the poorest of the poor.

In Daniel's case, his warfare lasted for three weeks with seemingly no answer. It was a warfare that had him fasting and praying for the welfare of his nation. Perhaps he did not realize it at the time, but his prayers were in the midst of the battle of two powerful superpowers that were vying for control of the world—powers that would eventually impact his people and his nation. His prayers were recognized and heard by the principalities and powers that were at war, beginning with the first day that he prayed.

While there was the changing of the guard of superpowers on earth, there was the changing of the principalities and powers in the heavens. The spiritual warfare found in Daniel 10 is revealed prior to this in the handwriting on the wall during Belshazzar's feast in Daniel 5. It shows the result of this struggle. Babylon was ready to fall to Persia. Through his prayers, Daniel had an immense part in this warfare and the development of this change. This struggle was taking place not only on earth, but in the heavens.

While Daniel was praying in chapter ten, the heavens would have been filled with the princes of principalities and powers. The Bible says that the prince of Persia that was to be the dominating force of the next superpower to come withstood this spiritual messenger that was on his way to speak to Daniel. This powerful struggle in the heavens delayed him, but he persisted, and stood firm against him. In other words, he fought against him. That's why he was delayed for three weeks in bringing an answer to Daniel. Once again, it was Michael the archangel who stands up for the people of Israel, and who came to the aid of this spiritual messenger and warrior so that he could deliver an answer to Daniel as he prayed out of his concern for his people.

In the development of spiritual warfare in our lives, it is up to us not only to get involved with the prayers that affect our lives personally, but to understand the warfare that affects the nations and peoples of the world. Daniel's prayer was connecting to a powerful warfare in the heavens that was going on even as he was praying.

In our own personal prayer struggle, we should not be discouraged when there seems to be a delay in answers to our prayers. God is always there for us, but we may sometimes wonder whether or not God will answer us. Answers to our prayers may take days, weeks, months, or even years. We may wonder if God is concerned about us at all. But the Bible makes it clear that we should not be impatient. It encourages us:

> Then He spoke a parable to them that men always ought to pray and not lose heart (Luke 18:1).

> And let us not grow weary while doing good, for in due season we shall reap if we do not lose heart (Galatians 6:9).

The messenger who was sent to Daniel was given the task of explaining what would happen to the nation of Israel at that moment. More importantly, he was there to tell Daniel what would happen to Israel in the latter days. Daniel got involved with a massive spiritual struggle for his nation.

Again, Daniel's prayer connected with changes that were happening with the forces of principalities and powers in the heavens which had great impact on what was happening on the earth at that time. As a result, Daniel's prayers got involved with the spiritual warfare of the nations that would affect the world hundreds of years into the future. These prayers got involved with forces of change in the heavens that would eventually affect changes on the earth.

It was revealed to Daniel that he had been warring with the prince of Persia, who was the up-and-coming principality and force that would rule that nation and that part of the world in the spirit and physical realms. He said that after that, years into the future he was going to be warring with the prince of Greece. This was the principality and the force that would rule that part of the world in the spirit and physical realm after the nation of Persia. Therefore Daniel's prayer was part of the spiritual warfare that involved not only Babylon and Persia who ruled in his lifetime. According to the words of the messenger, Daniel's prayer was also involved with the future nation of Greece, hundreds of years into the future, far beyond his lifetime.

The actual physical and political scene at the time of his prayer was the beginning of the fall of Babylon and the rise of the Media-Persia Empire. As mentioned earlier, this political power shift can clearly be seen earlier in Daniel 5 with the handwriting on the wall during the reign of Belshazzar of Babylon. Daniel interpreted the handwriting and told Belshazzar that the time of the kingdom of Babylon which he was ruling was over. Darius the Mede who had an alliance with the Persian Empire marched into Babylon and took over the kingdom.

It was absolutely essential for Babylon to fall because they would have never allowed the Jews to return to their land. Too much power and pride was at stake for them to let them go. It was similar to the time when Pharaoh would not let the children of Israel go during the time of Moses. The collapse of Babylon was necessary so that the Persians could come to power. It was King Cyrus of Persia who allowed the Jews to return to their beloved land. The kindness of this great king is seen in 2 Chronicles 36:22-23, Ezra 1:1-4, Isaiah 44:28 and 45:1-5.

As we pray for the nations, it is up to us to try and find out what God's will is for them, and pray that God's hand moves on their behalf. We need to focus on the spiritual warfare that God is having with the Devil over the issues of authority and power and continually worship God "in spirit and in truth." God looks for individuals who will pray and move His hand for mercy and grace; and as we will see through the ministry of Jeremiah, to build and plant nations, and to pull down and destroy nations. This kind of prayer is not just for the authorities over the nations, but can affect the dynamics of the church worldwide. It affects how easy the gospel can be preached, and whether or not the church can literally survive in some parts of the world. And like Daniel, sometimes our prayers can affect the changes in nations, years into the future.

Finally, in Daniel chapter 12, we read the following remarkable passage that we can define as the final and ultimate power struggle in the area of spiritual warfare during the time of the great tribulation. Changes come as trouble comes to the nations of the world. As quoted in the previous chapter, this passage makes it clear that Michael the archangel, the great prince of angels, is the one who stands up for the children of Israel. He is the guardian of God's people, Israel, and he is the one who wars with Satan over them in Revelation 12. I believe that he will be the one who will stand up to protect the children of Israel during the great tribulation. It is with amazement that we read these verses that show that the purpose for this tribulation is to bring the nation of Israel back to Him:

> And at that time shall Michael stand up, the great prince which standeth for the children of thy people: and there shall be a time of trouble, such as never was since there was a nation even to that same time: and at that time thy people shall be delivered, every one that shall be found written in the book. And many of them that sleep in the dust of the earth shall awake, some to everlasting life, and some to shame and everlasting contempt. And they that be wise shall shine as the brightness of the firmament; and they that turn many to righteousness as the stars forever and ever. But thou, O Daniel, shut up the words, and seal the book, even to the time of the end: many shall run to and fro, and knowledge shall be increased (Daniel 12:1-4 KJV).

EZEKIEL

Mysteriously, God needs someone who will appeal to Him and pray in order to bring mercy and righteousness to the land. During the days of Ezekiel, God was looking for a prayer warrior who would be like Moses and stay the hand of God. The children of Israel were in captivity and God was trying to explain to Ezekiel that He had needed someone to cry to Him to spare the land from destruction while they were still in Israel. Ezekiel was the prophet, but God needed a group of people or even a person other than this God-fearing messenger to intercede for the land. God couldn't find anyone.

The people were adulterous and sinful. They worshiped idols and disobeyed the true God. They oppressed the poor and needy and did nothing to aid the stranger in their midst. The prophets were in a conspiracy against the people. They ravaged souls for profit and gain. They had neglected the widows. They made no distinction between good and evil, nor the holy and the profane. They attempted to speak for God without a true word from Him. They had nothing in their hearts that spoke through their souls and to the people.

During the days of Ezekiel, the battle for dominance in the arena of spiritual warfare was clearly in favor of evil principalities and powers. We know that God wins the total war in the end of time but on this occasion, evil won the day. Their influence had completely overwhelmed any righteousness and holiness in the hearts of the people. For this, God was very displeased and the southern kingdom of Israel was taken into captivity. The case for the goodness and welfare of the children of Israel was in a sad state. Again, God could not find anyone who would intercede for the nation:

> So I sought for a man among them who would make a wall, and stand in the gap before Me on behalf of the land, that I should not destroy it; but I found no one (Ezekiel 22:30).

The message of Ezekiel was involving whether or not Israel would survive as a nation; and if it did, would they survive as a whole and healthy nation? Would God bring them back to their land in the latter days? According to Ezekiel 37, God was going to raise the nation of Israel in the latter days, similar to when bones in a graveyard would be resurrected and live. In the natural that would be impossible, but that passage of Scripture shows the winds of heaven coming and breathing into them for the resurrection of the nation. In this ongoing prophetic utterance, the rebuilding of that nation has happened again and again. The unconditional promise of God for the continued life of Israel in Genesis has repeatedly fit, and continues to fit any time in history, even in the latter days.

In 38 and 39, all of the goodness of this great act in new life for the nation will end in physical warfare and strife as the land of Israel is invaded during the time of the great tribulation. The armies of nations, called Gog and Magog, will play a leading role as they and other nations from the north invade Israel. This spiritual warfare will only end in catastrophe for these nations as the book of Ezekiel ends with a beautiful restoration of a new temple in Jerusalem as the nation of Israel entering into the millennium with a powerful and vast leadership role. Spiritual warfare for the nation of Israel will be won as both Isaiah and Micah wrote regarding this wonderful and glorious time in the future.

> The word that Isaiah the son of Amoz saw concerning Judah and Jerusalem. Now it shall come to pass in the latter days that the mountain of the Lord's house shall be established on the top of the mountains, and shall be exalted above the hills; and all nations shall flow to it. Many people shall come and say, "Come, and let us go up to the mountain of the Lord, to the house of the God of Jacob; He will teach us His ways, and we shall walk in His paths." For out of Zion shall go forth the law, and the word of the Lord from Jerusalem. He shall judge between the nations, and rebuke many people; they shall beat their swords into plowshares, and their spears into pruning hooks; nation shall not lift up sword against nation, neither shall they learn war anymore (Isaiah 2:1-4).

JEREMIAH

Jeremiah was a prophet who shed some interesting light on how a nation could turn from their evil ways and serve the true and living God. His mission and calling was to be a mouthpiece for God and to speak what God commanded him to speak. What he declared in Jeremiah 1 was the essence of his calling to preach to the nations; it says that God knew about him even before he was born. He was not to be afraid of those who would oppose him because God had put His words in Jeremiah's mouth.

God gave Jeremiah absolute authority to be a messenger who would either build up nations or destroy them. Spiritual warfare involves the nations; one nation may dominate the world for a time, but then another one will come into power. Our prayers tie into that scenario and we have a part in praying certain nations through to victory and others to failure. What an awesome and terrifying position to be in, but Jeremiah had to obey the calling of God in his life. Jeremiah was a spokesperson for God and he was in the position to tell his people that God was in control of the nations. In Jeremiah 1:10, it says how God would use Jeremiah:

> See, I have this day set thee over the nations and over the kingdoms, to root out and to pull down, to destroy and to throw down, to build and to plant.

The story of the potter and the clay in Jeremiah 18 further reveals God's dealing with the nations of the world. It is a story that is often used in realizing how God can remake us anew to serve Him. Many of us use this passage to show how we were far away from God, but God had to remake us like pottery and bring us back to Him. It's fine to use it personally, but that's a mistake we sometimes make in spiritual warfare. We focus everything on ourselves. If you take a closer look at the passage, it deals with the nation of Israel and with the nations of the world. God has a message for the nations: if they are on the course of evil but repent, God will deal kindly with them. However, if they start off well with God but turn to evil, God will punish them. The choice belongs to each nation.

> "O house of Israel, can I not do with you as this potter?" says the Lord. "Look, as the clay is in the potter's hand, so are you in my hand, O house of Israel! The instant I speak concerning a nation and concerning a kingdom, to pluck up, to pull down, and to destroy it, if that nation against whom I have spoken turns from its evil, I will relent of the disaster that I thought to bring upon it. And the instant I speak concerning a nation and concerning a kingdom, to build and to plant it, if it does evil in My sight so that it does not obey My voice, then I will relent concerning the good with which I said I would benefit it (Jeremiah 18:6-10).

Spiritual warfare in the book of Jeremiah was all about the attitude of the people of God, His chosen people of Israel. Jeremiah was a prophet whom no one wanted to hear. All of the other prophets were telling the people and the political leaders that everything was going to be all right. Jeremiah was saying just the opposite. He was telling all of them that the invading armies of Babylon were coming and it was too late for them to do anything about it. His voice was saying that they might just as well go along with what was about to happen. It was too late; there was nothing that God's people could do to prevent the destruction of their nation. Their disobedience was too far gone. They were disobedient for too long. The time for repentance was past; judgment was on its way. Jeremiah paid the price for his message through isolation and imprisonment. Again, spiritual warfare had taken a turn in favor of the evil messengers of ungodliness. The Devil was victorious in this battle but again, of course we know that God wins the war! Does the same thing hold true for the United States? Are we too far gone as a nation that is full of disobedience that there may never be the chance of recovery? Are we not heeding the messages of Ezekiel and Jeremiah? God help us!

BIRTH OF JESUS

At the time of the birth of Jesus there was a terrible assault against the God of heaven as the Devil tried to eliminate Jesus before He even had a chance to live His life and enter His ministry. The story of the birth of Christ is found in the gospels and it is the gospel of Matthew that gives us a clear look at the sinister plot against the promised Messiah.

Matthew tells us that wise men followed a star from the Middle East and came to worship the Messiah. They had come from the area of old Persia where much tradition was written about a future messianic king who was to be born in Israel. No doubt much of this tradition was left in that part of the world because of the influence of the children of Israel when they had been in captivity in that land for seventy years, which was about 500 to 600 years prior to this. This information about a future great king to be born in Israel would have been taught there during the time of Daniel when he was in Babylon.

At the birth of Christ it was Herod, the awful Roman-appointed ruler of Israel, who was enraged with a furious jealousy when he thought that his kingdom was threatened by the birth of the little child Jesus. His rage became a bold and broad spiritual battle that involved more than just Herod and the wise men. It involved more than Joseph and Mary having the experience of raising a child in a difficult period of time in history. It was an all-out war between God and the Devil over the master plan that God was instituting that would save the world from hell and total destruction.

We know the Scripture in the gospel of Matthew very well. An angel appeared to Joseph and told him that he and Mary needed to flee into Egypt in order to protect Jesus from being murdered. After Herod died, they were able to return to Israel.

The story that emerged in the pages of the sacred text shows a powerful battle that engaged God and the Devil—one of the greatest spiritual battles of all time. Nothing is said in Matthew about demons or principalities and powers in this story, but we can be sure that this was what was working behind the scenes. This is what is always at work—even though no references are made about it. The Devil is always attempting to nullify or thwart the plans of God at any given opportunity.

It is always in the mind of the Devil to tackle the God of heaven who kicked him out of His very throne room. Even though his demise as "the anointed cherub who covers" happened just before the time of creation—or possibly eons before that time—he hasn't forgotten or changed his tactics since then. He wants the worship that is supposed to be attributed to God to be directed toward him.

The Devil wished to destroy the plans that God had instituted as long ago as the garden of Eden when he tempted Adam and Eve to sin. In the case of Adam and Eve, God had an immediate recovery plan for redemption and that plan set in motion a timetable for warfare that the human race has not escaped from since. It is recorded in Genesis 3:15 as God told the Devil at that time:

> And I will put enmity between you and the woman, and between your seed and her Seed; He shall bruise your head, and you shall bruise His heel.

This was the first prophetic Scripture of the promised Messiah. This was the promise of the Messiah that eventually led to the horrifying spiritual warfare at the birth of Jesus that saw thousands of babies killed in an attempt by the Devil to secure the death of the Son of God. This single act was the Devil's plan to destroy this engaging promise of redemption and salvation immediately after man fell into sin.

In that passage in Genesis, we see the unfolding of God's messianic plan. God's answer was that through the very woman that the temptation of sin first came, from her seed would come the plan of the Messiah, the cross and redemption. Out of Eve's sin came the experience of the birth of deliverance. This is the first revelation of God's mercy, grace, and love after the first sin and it came through Eve, the first sinner.

Just like her, no matter how badly we may ruin things in life, out of ruin and out of our sin we can find recovery, and God will have mercy. Out of disgrace we can have redemption and deliverance. No matter to what degree we may personally have messed things up, we can look to God who lives within us, and He can bring us answers from the very pain and shame of the sin itself.

God can continue to use the very people who have slipped and fallen into sin by offering them a second chance to redeem themselves. Eve was the first human to be tempted, to fall into sin, but she was also the first human to know God's plan for a Redeemer who would rescue her from her sin—as well as all of fallen humankind. God's mercy, grace, and love are so powerful and wonderful! May God be praised forever and ever!

If you examine that text in Genesis 3, the crushing fatal blow that was to eventually ruin the work of the Devil and the power that he would have in this warfare against God Himself was announced. His head was to receive a fatal blow. He was doomed. He is destined for the lake of Fire. The text also shows that God would allow a Messiah to be harmed with what was eventually revealed as His death on the cross of Calvary to redeem humankind. That is the meaning of the phrase that His heel would be bruised. God Himself would pay the price in order to save His creation.

Through this Scripture in Genesis, we can see that the enmity was set. The warfare that was between God and the Devil had fallen to the earth. The division between the hordes of followers of the Devil and the offspring of the woman Eve was now in place. This beginning warfare on earth in Genesis would rage a terrible storm throughout Judaism and the entire Old Testament. This included the time through the birth of Jesus Christ, Son of God, Messiah, King of Kings, and Lord of Lords, as the Devil through Herod, tried to destroy Him.

The life of Jesus Christ was one that was to bring glory to God the Father. It was to bring peace on earth and goodwill. The life of Jesus would be filled with miracles, healings, and the filling of men and women with hope as He battled the works of the Devil.

THE TEMPTATION OF JESUS

Jesus encountered the most severe of all testing. He had a direct and face-to-face encounter with the Devil himself. This was the epic and classic struggle involving fasting and prayer and then His temptation, as the Devil zeroed in on one of His weakest moments. The Bible says that Jesus fasted for forty days and nights and then became hungry. He was led by the Spirit of God to be tempted by the Devil. Being led by the Spirit when you are encountering principalities and powers during a time of temptation is the best way. The temptation was in three areas that the apostle John mentions, and involved our love and fascination with this life as opposed to the adoration that we should have for our heavenly Father:

> Do not love the world or the things in the world. If anyone loves the world, the love of the Father is not in

him. For all that is in the world—the lust of the flesh, the lust of the eyes, and the pride of life—is not of the Father but is of the world. And the world is passing away, and the lust of it; but he who does the will of God abides forever (1 John 2:15-17).

This was just like the temptation of Adam and Eve in Genesis 3. Eve was tempted with the lust of the flesh because the tree was good for food. She was tempted with the lust of the eyes because the tree was pleasant looking. She was tempted with the pride of life because she felt that the tree would make her wise. The Devil enticed Eve to eat from the tree in the middle of the garden of Eden because she thought it would give her the knowledge of both good and evil and that she would be as the gods:

And when the woman saw that the tree was good for food, and that it was pleasant to the eyes, and a tree to be desired to make one wise, she took of the fruit thereof, and did eat, and gave also unto her husband with her; and he did eat (Genesis 3:6 KJV).

These were the same issues that Jesus encountered. He was tempted in the lust of the flesh by being tempted by the Devil to turn stones to bread so that He could eat. Eating bread would have been the most natural thing to do after a fast, but having the Devil lure Him to do so would have been giving in to demonic forces. Turning stones to bread was not what the Spirit of God would have led Him to do. This clearly would have been seeing stones and lusting after them to satisfy the flesh rather than finding the proper means to end the fast through the strength that His Father in heaven provided. When we end a fast, we should carefully come off the fast by the leading of the Holy Spirit through continued prayer and not through the fulfillment of our natural craving for food. Jesus' answer to the Devil in Luke is a quote from Deuteronomy 8:3:

> But Jesus answered him, saying, "It is written, '*Man
> shall not live by bread alone, but by every word of God'*"
> (Luke 4:4).

Then Jesus was tempted in the lust of the eyes by having the Devil show Him the kingdoms of the world, saying that he would let Jesus have them if only Jesus would worship him. The Devil had no authority to offer Him the kingdoms because the kingdoms of this world belong to God, and are under His control. They are only under the Devil's influence with God's permission. The Devil overstepped his boundaries. Of course, Jesus refused to worship the Devil because His allegiance was to His Father in heaven, and because He knew to whom those kingdoms really belonged. He also knew that worship was the crux of spiritual warfare.

This is where we too should know to whom the power of the kingdoms of this world really belongs and not be fooled by the trickery of the Devil. Make no mistake about it—the kingdoms of the earth belong to God as it says in Psalms 24:1, "The earth is the Lord's and the fullness thereof; the world, and they that dwell therein" (KJV). Jesus' answer to the Devil in Luke is a quote from Deuteronomy 6:13:

> And Jesus answered and said to him, "Get behind Me,
> Satan! For it is written, '*You shall worship the Lord your
> God, and Him only you shall serve'*" (Luke 4:8).

The third temptation with which Jesus was tempted was the pride of life. The Devil brought Jesus to the top of the temple and enticed Him to cast Himself down to the ground because God's angels were sure to protect Him. The Devil even mentioned the Scripture in Psalms 91:11-12 to support his temptation which is quoted in Luke "He shall give His angels charge over you, to keep you...in their hands they shall bear you up, lest you dash your foot against a stone" (Luke 4:10-11). The Devil conveniently left out the phrase "in all thy ways." To be sure, if one is to be kept in all their ways, it does not involve attempting to commit suicide or committing sin. It should be the ways that God leads us in that would bring Him glory and praise, not violence and destruction.

Our mission should be as Christ's was—to submit to God, resisting the Devil. When we resist the Devil, the Devil will flee from us.

Jesus, of course, knew better. He knew that it would be a mistake to put Himself in a position to purposefully do Himself bodily harm and to force His Father in heaven to protect Him in an unnatural situation. This is where pride can enter into the heart so that a person would even imagine that they could attempt something like this in their own power. Jesus' answer to the Devil is a quote from Deuteronomy 6:16:

> And Jesus answered and said to him, *"It has been said,
> 'You shall not tempt the Lord your God'"* (Luke 4:12).

All three of these temptations were in the realm of possibility for Christ to accomplish because He had the power to bring all three of them to pass. He had the power to turn stones to bread. He could have worshiped whom He wanted—God or the Devil—but of course, He would have never worshiped the Devil. He could have easily floated to the ground from the top of the temple under the protection of His own power. However, in all three of these temptations, Jesus easily repelled them by the working of the Holy Spirit in His life and by the power of the Word of God. He knew His mission in life and whom He was to obey and serve. He had entered into the battleground where His Father in heaven did battle with the Devil and He won! Jesus passed the spiritual warfare test!

THE GARDEN AND THE CROSS

The garden of Gethsemane experience for Christ and His disciples was crucial and pivotal in God's redemptive plan and one of absolute amazement as it relates to spiritual warfare. Christ knew what the plan was and why He came into this world: to give the opportunity to men and women everywhere to come to God and miss the path of loss and ruin in hell.

The spiritual warfare that Christ was to pass through so that salvation could keep us from hell was one of the greatest tests He had to endure.

Before the mockery of His trial, before having His reputation exchanged with the criminal Barabbas, before the embarrassment of being crucified between thieves, He had to engage in spiritual warfare. He could have walked away from it if He had so desired. The cross was looming as big as life in front of Him.

His own disciples were of no help or support, as they fell asleep during the most critical hours of spiritual warfare. They didn't yet understand, and they didn't have the stamina to carry them through the night of watching and prayer. Their colossal failure would have to wait until after the Resurrection of Christ for them to have spiritual victory and the resolve to carry out the plan of salvation which was to be for all humankind.

The Bible says that in that garden, Jesus could have called legions of angels from the spirit world to annihilate His physical enemies and deliver Him at this critical hour. But His warfare was not with the physical world. It was not about overcoming the physical battle or problems that He was going through. His fight was all-out spiritual warfare with His Father's enemy, the Devil. While in the garden of Gethsemane, He knew that this physical action of arrest and embarrassment needed to happen in order that Scripture could be fulfilled. While on the cross, He even cried out to His Father to forgive His killers because they did not know what they were doing.

Jesus was caught in the warfare between His Father who sent Him as the "only begotten Son" to die for the sins of the world, and His Father's greatest enemy, the Devil, who would have loved to end Christ's life and career right then and there. The spiritual warfare between His Father and the Devil was that the Devil wanted worship to be diverted from the Father to himself as seen during Christ's temptation in the wilderness at the beginning of His ministry. That's the essence of all spiritual warfare that we encounter here on earth. To whom will we give worship and praise? To whom do we swear our heart's allegiance?

My difficulties and trials that I may have here on earth are only secondary to the premise of giving glory to God! I must not let my mind be diverted by my engagement into personal dilemmas and difficulties, no matter how harsh they may be. True, my trials involve the Devil and all the principalities and powers that fight against me. Like Job, I may lose many things here on earth, but I must fight through them in order to give glory and praise to God who has already won the victory! That's the fight!

The plan of mercy and redemption for the world could have been lost just hours before the cross in that garden where Jesus was praying. The suffering of the flesh and the emotional and psychological stress that He was under was identified by Him as a "cup," and it seems as if He wasn't so sure that He could drink from it. It was a cup of pain and suffering, laced with the sin and hopelessness of all humankind that He had to drink if He was to fulfill His Father's will. His holiness and righteousness caused Him to want to pull back from the dredges of that cup, but thank God, He said, "Not my will, but Thy will, be done."

In this case, what the Devil should have done was run! Run away as far as possible from this encounter with Christ. Run as far away from this master plan of redemption of which he knew nothing about and did not understand. Run with his tail between his legs. This was about to be a real loss for him. He never should have entered Judas on the night of the celebration of the Passover with Jesus and the rest of the disciples. He never should have conspired to have Judas plan the execution of Christ because the cross was about to be the death blow to his head that Genesis 3:15 was talking about. It was to be the finishing, decisive, powerful, and pivotal stroke that was the beginning of the end for the Devil.

The problem for the Devil and his demon helpers is that they did not understand the plan of God—that from the seed of death would come the reaping of life for anyone who would believe in the resurrection power of Christ. The Devil was still too enticed by the possibility that all the worship was to be his if only he could kill the Son of God and thwart God's plan. This made him bloodthirsty, blind, and drunk with revenge for being thrown out of heaven so he stood behind the plan to end it once and for all at the cross. By having a part in killing Christ, he thought he had won the victory and it was over for the plan of God and the Son of God. He apparently thought that Christ's death was the end of it all.

In the darkness that surrounded the cross, the disciples thought they had lost and the Devil thought that he had won. I'm sure the Devil was confident, but little did he realize that it was just the beginning, because the resurrection was just three days after Christ's death on the cross. He was in for the fight of his life that will only end when he is finally cast into the lake of fire mentioned in Revelation 20:10. His ignorance about the wonderful plan of God is clearly seen in what Paul the apostle wrote about:

> But we speak the wisdom of God in a mystery, the hidden wisdom which God ordained before the ages for our glory, which none of the rulers of this age knew; for had they known, they would not have crucified the Lord of glory. But as it is written: "Eye has not seen, nor ear heard, nor have entered into the heart of man, the things which God hath prepared for those who love Him" (1 Corinthians 2:7-9).

The Devil just didn't understand the redemptive plan of God. In the end of all things, it is Jesus Christ who is the ultimate authority over all principalities and powers. He has the greatest jurisdiction and control in the universe. He is above every spiritual force and it is His will that created all things and that holds them together by the Word of His power:

> For by Him all things were created that are in heaven and that are on earth, visible and invisible, whether thrones or dominions or principalities or powers. All things were created through Him and for Him. And He is before all things, and in Him all things consist (Colossians 1:16-17).

> Who being the brightness of His glory and the express image of His person, and upholding all things by the word of His power, when He had by Himself purged our sins, sat down at the right hand of the Majesty on high (Hebrews 1:3).

Intergalactic Warfare

The Bible says that God the Father has placed Christ above all these authorities and we are seated above these authorities with Him. This is what gives us our authority in the spiritual realm:

> Which He worked in Christ when He raised Him from the dead and seated Him at His right hand in the heavenly places, far above all principality and power and might and dominion, and every name that is named, not only in this age but also in that which is to come. And He put all things under His feet, and gave Him to be head over all things to the church (Ephesians 1:20-22).

> And raised us up together, and made us sit together in the heavenly places in Christ Jesus, that in the ages to come He might show the exceeding riches of His grace in His kindness toward us in Christ Jesus (Ephesians 2:6-7).

The Bible says about Christ in Philippians 3:10 that we can "know Him and the power of His resurrection." How can knowing Christ and the power of His resurrection, an event that happened nearly 2,000 years ago, help me today? What it does for me is that it becomes my power to rebuke the Devil because the Devil cannot give me resurrection. Only Christ can! That's the victory! I can say to the Devil, "I'm sticking with Christ. Get behind me. You have no power to raise me from the dead. Therefore I won't live for you, I won't serve you, nor will I worship you. I will live for the one who can raise me to eternal life and grant to me the blessings of an eternal relationship of a loving and caring God. I will have a new home in the new heaven and new earth." That's what gives me my boldness and might against the Devil to resist him so that he will flee, and that becomes "the power of the resurrection" for me and for others who believe.

We must rest in the conclusion that we belong to God because of what Christ has done for us and offered to us. We have eternal life because Christ gave His life in substitution for our death when He died on the cross for our sins. Jesus paid the price so that we may have that resurrection power. This is what we must continue to believe and rest in; we must continue to remind the Devil of the resurrection power we have in Christ. The battle that the Devil puts us through in this life can in no way compare to the eternal life that God offers to us. There is an eternal peaceful home in heaven waiting for us. The Devil only offers us hopelessness and separation from God. God offers us eternal life that is beyond the capability of what the Devil can offer. God reigns supreme. To God be praised!

Chapter Three: Why God Uses Prayer and Spiritual Warfare

WHY GOD NEEDS PEOPLE TO PRAY

In order to understand prayer and spiritual warfare, it would be wise to try to find out which part of our being communicates with God. Which part of us is the part that prays? We can discover that if we examine what we are made of. Science has revealed that the same chemical elements that are in the soil of the earth are found in the human body. We have a body because God took elements from the ground and created it. We are a living soul because God breathed His Spirit into Adam's body. The dust of the earth that formed the body and the Spirit that was God-breathed into Adam were united to form the soul. God made us into the three components of body, soul, and spirit.

> And the Lord God formed man of the dust of the ground,
> and breathed into his nostrils the breath of life; and man
> became a living being (Genesis 2:7).

It's easy to understand that we have a body and what it is that makes up our body, but it is very difficult to define the difference between the soul and the spirit. That's because we sometimes interpret the soul and the spirit interchangeably. In my view, man became a soul by the infusion of God's Spirit into the body. In other words, it was the pairing of the spirit and the body that defined and formed the soul. There would be no soul without the spirit and the body. The soul is therefore the outgrowth of the spirit and the body and is the middle ground between these two human and spiritual entities.

Also in the middle ground, as part of the soul, is the human mind that gives us our consciousness and awareness. Along with the soul, it is the mind that helps to bring about the expressions of the body and the spirit. Through our mind comes our intelligence and understanding which help us to reason, think, perceive, and judge. It behooves us to develop a spiritual mind as opposed to a carnal fleshly mind.

> For those who live according to the flesh set their minds on the things of the flesh, but those who live according to the Spirit, the things of the Spirit. For to be carnally minded is death, but to be spiritually minded is life and peace. Because the carnal mind is enmity against God; for it is not subject to the law of God, nor indeed can be (Romans 8:5-7).

The things that we express to others that come from our mind and through our soul are such things as experience, passion, emotions, imagination, conscience, memory, reason, affections, the will, and the intellect. These types of manifestations of the soul can be seen as coming from either the body or the spirit as both of them have the ability to be the basis for them. From the body can come any of those issues just mentioned that we express through the soul, and from the spirit can come any of those issues just mentioned that we also express through the soul. The body can emotionally send those expressions through the soul, and the spirit can supernaturally send those expressions through the soul as well. We can live in the flesh and express sin through our soul, or we can live in the Spirit and express godliness through our soul. Both the body and the spirit can formulate these expressions which is why we often have that tug of war between the flesh and the spirit that the Bible talks about. We can read about this dichotomy of the body and spirit in Matthew and Galatians:

> Watch and pray, that ye enter not into temptation: the spirit indeed is willing, but the flesh is weak (Matthew 26:41 KJV).

86

> This I say then, Walk in the Spirit, and ye shall not fulfil the lust of the flesh. For the flesh lusteth against the Spirit, and the Spirit against the flesh: and these are contrary the one to the other: so that ye cannot do the things that ye would (Galatians 5:16-17 KJV).

We therefore can determine that it is the spirit that prays and communicates with God through the soul. It is not the flesh that communicates with God. Therefore, our spirit must be in tune with God, and we must attempt to control every aspect of the flesh to which we so easily succumb. Again, the soul is the gateway that reflects both our body and our spirit. If we fall prey to the soul's activities that appeal to our flesh, we will further alienate ourselves from God. If we allow the soul to appeal to our spirit that is in tune with God, we can draw closer to Him.

> For those who live according to the flesh set their minds on the things of the flesh, but those who live according to the Spirit, the things of the Spirit. For to be carnally minded is death, but to be spiritually minded is life and peace (Romans 8:5-6).

> And if Christ be in you, the body is dead because of sin; but the Spirit is life because of righteousness. But if the Spirit of him that raised up Jesus from the dead dwell in you, he that raised up Christ from the dead shall also quicken your mortal bodies by his Spirit that dwelleth in you (Romans 8:10-11 KJV).

Sometimes an individual's spirit is under the control of, or possessed by, an evil spirit that either enters or binds that person. In the gospel of Mark, Jesus had a great opportunity to teach His disciples about casting out demonic spirits and what it would take to be successful at it. In the ninth chapter, a father brought his demoniac son to Jesus whose evil spirit in him was literally trying to destroy his son's body. The disciples lacked the authority to cast out the evil spirit, so Jesus rebuked His disciples for a lack of power to do so. Jesus successfully cast out the evil spirit. When His disciples asked why they could not cast out the evil spirit, Jesus' answer came right to the heart of dealing with principalities and powers—fasting! Jesus encouraged the father concerning his faith, and He admonished his disciples for the power they lacked. This is what Jesus said to them both:

> If you can believe, all things are possible to him that believes (Mark 9:23).

> This kind can come out by nothing but prayer and fasting (Mark 9:29).

Why fasting when it comes to trying to overcome spirits in the world of principalities and powers? The answer is that when we are living according to the flesh, the focus of our lives is on ourselves. Fasting takes the focus off of the pleasures of our flesh. Food is one of the last things, if not the very last thing, that any of us would give up when it comes to satisfying the flesh. We are willing to give up many other personal items, but food is an absolute necessity if we are to stay alive. Therefore fasting will carry great weight when we are wrestling with principalities and powers. When we fast, these powers realize that we mean business. If we are willing to give up the very last thing that brings total satisfaction to our flesh, the very thing that will keep us alive, they quickly come to the conclusion that we mean business and they hightail it and run. Fasting carries great power against the Devil and his demonic angels.

When we are living according to the spirit, the focus is off ourselves and on God's power and will. Fasting generates power with God, against the Devil and over self. It generates power in the Spirit because we are no longer gratifying the flesh. Then God will know, and also the Devil will know, that we are serious about what is important. Winning the battle over our own flesh plays a huge part in victory over principalities and powers.

That's why God's people need to pray because God has confined Himself not to act on behalf of His creation without the spiritual connection and the communication that He has with the spiritual side of man through prayer. God wants to appeal to us through our soul, but He wishes to connect to our spirit, and not our flesh. The reason God created man was because He wished to have created beings He could communicate with, and aid Him in His warfare with the Devil. Our fellowship with Him has to be with our spirit communing with God's Spirit through our soul. It is through this manner that we can connect with God to fight against the Devil in spiritual warfare. Again, the Bible says that God created man out of the dust of the earth and breathed His Spirit into him, and man became a living soul.

MOVING THE HAND OF GOD

There are a few things that must be in order if we want to make a major impact on the work of God, particularly in the realm of spiritual warfare. Anytime we do not see God move, it is usually, if not always, the fault of the person who is praying or who is being prayed for. It is not God's fault. One example as already mentioned in the New Testament was when God would not answer prayer for the apostle Paul when he wanted to be healed. God would not remove the thorn in his flesh because Paul knew that he might be filled with pride. He had to be careful because of the abundance of revelations that were given to him.

If we are to see God move in the area of spiritual warfare and authority, we must first of all remove any pride in our lives. There is no reason for human flesh to receive any glory. All glory must go to God and Him alone. Second, we must make sure that our motives are not for selfish gain. The apostle James tells us that sometimes we can ask amiss, in other words, ask for the wrong reasons. We may use God's answers for our own pleasure. Third, sometimes we operate our spiritual lives outside the boundaries of prayerfulness and dwell in prayerlessness. Communication with God must be of utmost importance even if it is only for a few minutes at a time. The apostle Paul said in 1 Thessalonians 5:17, "Pray without ceasing."

Intergalactic Warfare

All of our praying must be done with the understanding that the principalities and powers of the heavens hear what we pray. As we pray and praise God for all of His attributes such as His magnificence, grace, fullness, perfection, redemption, power, and forgiveness, the angels of the heavenly realm hear us. This is what gives us our power as we declare our praise to God because they know what we are saying. We are to remind them, make known to them, and continue to reveal to them who and what God is, and declare all of His wonderful attributes that were given to His church. Concerning the responsibility of the church and prayer, the Bible says:

> [The purpose is] that *through the church the complicated, many-sided wisdom of God in all its infinite variety and innumerable aspects might now be made known to the angelic rulers and authorities* (principalities and powers) in the heavenly sphere. This is in accordance with the terms of the eternal and timeless purpose which He has realized and carried into effect in [the person of] Christ Jesus our Lord, in Whom, because of our faith in Him, we dare to have the boldness (courage and confidence) of free access (an unreserved approach to God with freedom and without fear) (Ephesians 3:10 AMP).

Sometimes spiritual warfare takes a turn that no one can expect. We see this even in the life of Jesus when He encountered unbelief in the people to whom He was trying to minister. In the gospel of Mark, we can see at least three reasons why Jesus could do no miracles in some cases. First of all was the familiarity of the people who knew Him. This showed a severe lack of respect for His calling and ministry. Sometimes ministers face this same complexity. Second, they were offended by Him. This revealed a jealousy that they freely expressed. Third, there was their lack of faith that caused amazement from Jesus.

There was something lost in this battle in the realm of spiritual warfare that even prevented Jesus from doing His mighty works. Just like Jesus, sometimes we are unable to do the works of healing and miracles because of the spiritual warfare we encounter. Additionally, sometimes the gifts of healing and miracles are given only to those who are God-called to this type of ministry. In the case of Jesus in the gospel of Mark, the only thing that He was able to do was to lay His hands on a few sick people and heal them. This story is in Mark 6:

> Then He went out from there and came to His own country, and His disciples followed Him. And when the Sabbath had come, He began to teach in the synagogue. And many hearing Him were astonished, saying, "Where did this Man get these things? And what wisdom is this which is given to Him, that such mighty works are performed by His hands! Is this not the carpenter, the Son of Mary, and brother of James, Joses, Judas, and Simon? And are not His sisters here with us?" So they were offended at Him. But Jesus said to them, "A prophet is not without honor except in his own country, among his own relatives, and in his own house." Now He could do no mighty work there, except that He laid His hands on a few sick people and healed them. And He marveled because of their unbelief (Mark 6:1-6).

The conclusion to this story is that in order to see the hand of God move in the realm of principalities and powers, we must first show the respect needed for the minister's calling and ministry. We cannot come against any individual who we know has been given the wisdom and authority that comes from God. If we are not sure of a person's ministry, we should first of all keep our mouth shut except in a case of doctrinal error or moral failure. Second, there must be no jealousy that would cause us to think that we could do better than the one who is doing the ministering. Third, our faith must always be in the position to be tapped by God to ensure the successful meeting of the needs of the people.

During the days of Moses, the children of Israel almost lost an important battle in the spiritual realm of principalities and powers because of their disobedience. It almost cost them their relationship with God. The Israelites made a golden calf in order to worship it and God wanted to destroy them. Moses had been on Mount Sinai receiving the commandments; and in a moment of wrath, God wanted to forget the promises He made to Abraham, Isaac, and Jacob. He told Moses that He wanted to make another nation that came from him. Moses pleaded with God not to destroy His people and God listened to Moses and had mercy on Israel. It was a close call, but that generation almost lost out on being a great nation for God. God's mercy was greater than the sin of the children of Israel as the pleading of Moses moved the hand of God. We see this remarkable story in Exodus:

> Then Moses pleaded with the Lord his God, and said: "Lord, why does Your wrath burn hot against Your people whom You have brought out of the land of Egypt with great power and with a mighty hand? Why should the Egyptians speak, and say, 'He brought them out to harm them, to kill them in the mountains, and to consume them from the face of the earth'? Turn from Your fierce wrath, and relent from this harm to Your people. Remember Abraham, Isaac, and Israel, Your servants, to whom You swore by Your own self, and said to them, 'I will multiply your descendants as the stars of heaven; and all this land that I have spoken of I give to your descendants, and they shall inherit it forever.'" So the Lord relented from the harm which He said He would do to His people (Exodus 32:11-14).

What would we do without the love, grace, and mercy of God? These attributes of God are so powerfully at work within those who have come to God through Christ that they are immeasurably endowed to every believer. There is an inner strength that God gives to the believer that aids us in our spiritual warfare, and that brings out an abundant power that works through us. We can be victorious in our warfare if we understand how wide, long, deep, and high God strengthens our inner spirit. Our strength to fight comes from God who has given us His fullness. Concerning the love of God and the inner strength we receive, Ephesians says this:

> That He would grant you, according to the riches of His glory, to be strengthened with might through His Spirit in the inner man, that Christ may dwell in your hearts through faith; that you, being rooted and grounded in love, may be able to comprehend with all the saints what is the width and length and depth and height—to know the love of Christ which passes knowledge; that you may be filled with all the fullness of God (Ephesians 3:16-19).

God's love is seen in His act of creation. It also appeals to us in His great love for the world. God is the one who sent His only son to die for man's sin. God's love is what we can rely on when we are involved with spiritual warfare because we know that it is His love that is in us that makes us bold enough to fight the battles of spiritual wickedness. As an example of God's love, He told us to love our enemies. By the same token, we are also to love the enemies of the gospel that God has given us to preach, even though we are commissioned to fight in the power of the Spirit with the principalities and powers that are behind them. Our physical enemies can also come to Christ as we pray for them. We are encouraged in this battle that we have weapons that are beyond those that are at our disposal in the flesh.

> For though we walk in the flesh, we do not war according to the flesh. For the weapons of our warfare are not carnal but mighty in God for pulling down strongholds, casting down arguments and every high thing that exalts itself against the knowledge of God, bringing every thought into captivity to the obedience of Christ, and being ready to punish all disobedience when your obedience is fulfilled (2 Corinthians 10:3-6).

Again, it is His love that emboldens us because we know that His love is eternal and that one day when we see Him, all of spiritual wickedness will be gone as it will be trampled under His feet. We are on the firing line and we are God's test for the accomplishments and victories of the spiritual warfare today so that we will enjoy victory with God in the future.

The love of God toward His created beings can be defined as tender and passionate affection. It is a benevolent attention that He takes pleasure in granting to His people. It is His love that we can be confident in every day that we serve Him. The following Scriptures about His love should encourage us.

> The Lord has appeared of old to me, saying: "Yes, I have loved you with an everlasting love; therefore with lovingkindness I have drawn you" (Jeremiah 31:3).

> Behold what manner of love the Father has bestowed on us, that we should be called children of God! Therefore the world does not know us, because it did not know Him (1 John 3:1).

God's grace is an endowment of a clemency or pardon. It is unmerited favor or immunity given to us because of Christ's sacrifice on the cross of Calvary. The word "grace" in acrostic form is **G**od's **R**iches **A**t **C**hrist's **E**xpense. It is **GRACE**! The following Scriptures on God's grace show us how unworthy we are.

> For the grace of God that brings salvation has appeared to all men, teaching us that, denying ungodliness and worldly lusts, we should live soberly, righteously, and godly in the present age (Titus 2:11-12).

> In Him we have redemption through His blood, the forgiveness of sins, according to the riches of His grace which He made to abound toward us in all wisdom and prudence (Ephesians 1:7-8).

God's mercy is understood to be an unusual compassionate and kind forbearance that is shown to the ones who have offended Him. It is His compassion or pity through which He expresses His love to us and through us. The following Scriptures reveal how far God has gone in expressing His mercy.

> But the mercy of the Lord is from everlasting to everlasting on those who fear Him, and His righteousness to children's children, to such as keep His covenant, and to those who remember His commandments to do them (Psalms 103:17-18).

> Through the Lord's mercies we are not consumed, because His compassions fail not. They are new every morning; great is Your faithfulness (Lamentations 3:22-23).

> Not by works of righteousness which we have done, but according to His mercy He saved us, through the washing of regeneration and renewing of the Holy Spirit (Titus 3:5).

It is His love, grace, and mercy that gives us the assurance we need in spiritual warfare. Relying on these gifts and other gifts of favor from God is what moves His hand as we serve Him in the spiritual battles that we fight and endure for Him. We have confidence that He is with us in our fight against spiritual wickedness in high places. This is what gives us the boldness to tackle any of the enemies of God who are there to try and prevent us from receiving all of God's goodness and blessing in our lives as God fights in His great warfare with the Devil.

THE PUZZLING CONCEPT OF PRAYER

Here are some questions that beg an answer. Why does God even need prayer? Why should God have even developed the need for prayer? Couldn't He have gotten along without depending on the weakness of humans in times of spiritual crisis and physical desperation for His people? Prayer is so dependent upon the spiritual strength of humans that if someone fails in prayer, the whole skeletal framework of prayer in any given case can be a disaster. In some instances, the spiritual house can literally fall apart. Victims of weakened forms of prayer can have their spiritual lives harmed through a lack of faith or interest in prayer.

Why should God depend on puny man to run this world? Isn't God sovereign and all-powerful so that He can accomplish whatsoever He wills? The truth is He spoke the universe into existence and then saddled the management of the world that He created upon conversations of prayer and communication to and from man, the ultimate work of His creation! This is where the Deist who rejects supernatural revelation from God misunderstands God and the relationship He has with His creation. The Deist believes in a God who created the world, but has remained indifferent to it since. We believe that God has placed a dependence of the direction of the world on how much a man or a woman will pray. He has tied Himself to the prayers and faith of individual worshipers, preachers, believers, and upon the total body of Christ.

God is self-sufficient, and He can accomplish anything His desire and will set out to do. Yet much of what He does, He does after man consults with Him through prayer; then God unleashes His power through that prayer. God has a master plan for the world, but He expects man to tap into an understanding of that plan, and break through to God in prayer, so that His hand would be moved. It's almost as if God has made Himself helpless without our prayers. Without that communication, He would not be Lord of His creation.

As already mentioned in the case of Ezekiel, God was looking for someone who would stay His hand so that He would not destroy the land of Israel. He loved Israel and He was looking for someone to love Him back enough so that they would convince God, their lover, that He should stop the onslaught of the invading armies against the nation of Israel. Also and similar to the situation with Moses, God needed someone to ask Him for the release of His mercy and forgiveness because of the severe disobedience of His people.

Why did God set up a system of prayer that many times is sure to fail because of man's unwillingness to do so? Why doesn't God just overlook what we fail to do and carry out what He wills? While Jesus was on the earth, He was very successful in the area of prayer and spiritual warfare. When He ascended back to His Father in heaven, He left to us the management of the church, as well as the management of the warfare to fight with the evil principalities and powers in the heavens. How amazing is that? Clearly, God wants us to step up to the plate and take leadership in this spiritual battle. Scripture does make it clear that all we need to do is ask of God and He will answer. In the gospel of John, it says:

> Most assuredly, I say to you, he who believes in Me, the works that I do he will do also; and greater works than these he will do, because I go to My Father. And whatever you ask in My name, that I will do, that the Father may be glorified in the Son. If you ask anything in My name, I will do it (John 14:12-14).

> If you abide in Me, and My words abide in you, you will ask what you desire, and it shall be done for you. By this My Father is glorified, that you bear much fruit; so you will be My disciples (John 15:7-8).

> Most assuredly, I say to you, whatever you ask the Father in My name He will give you. Until now you have asked nothing in My name. Ask, and you will receive, that your joy may be full (John 16:23-24).

There is a key to these Scriptures because of our entrance into spiritual warfare once we begin to believe for answers to prayer. We have the all-consuming power to "ask anything," "ask what you desire," and "ask, and you will receive." It seems like there is unlimited access into the throne room of God and He will give us anything and everything. But the same apostle John who wrote these astounding sentences of seemingly receiving anything that we pray for, is the same apostle who wrote years later that we must know God's will when we pray:

> Now this is the confidence that we have in Him, that if we *ask anything according to His will*, He hears us. And if we know that He hears us, whatever we ask, we

know that we have the petitions that we have asked of Him (1 John 5:14-15).

We must conclude that God will do hardly anything to benefit man without prayer and intercession from man himself in the area of spiritual warfare. The key, however, is to enter into that realm and discover what to pray and how to pray for certain things. The reason is that God is fighting against the Devil and we must discover what God is attempting to do and we must not pray contrary to what His actions are. Sometimes His actions toward nations are in the positive for growth and production, and sometimes His actions are in the negative as He deals with their sin and self-destruction. It is up to us to know what God's will is, and how to pray that will. John isn't the only one who mentions praying His will. The apostle Paul said:

> Likewise the Spirit also helps in our weaknesses. *For we do not know what we should pray for as we ought*, but the Spirit Himself makes intercession for us with groanings which cannot be uttered. Now He who searches the hearts knows what the mind of the Spirit is, because He makes intercession for the saints *according to the will of God* (Romans 8:26-27).

If we pray contrary to His will and design for our lives, it can be frustrating and debilitating. We can become fearful and discouraged. For our own personal prayers and needs, it is important to know how God is working out His will in our lives, in the lives of our families, and in the lives of our friends and coworkers. It is similar to what Job and the apostle Paul went through when God made them pass through the fires of difficulty. It is then that we can pray according to His will as we pass through certain circumstances that can lead us to victory.

More importantly, He also urges us to become involved with the warfare He has with the Devil. God wants us to take the lead in overcoming His archenemy, the Devil, because living souls are at stake who need to be brought into the kingdom of God. The Devil wants these souls just as much as God does. He is willing to fight until the bitter end to get what he wants. The earth is the battleground and we are stuck right in the middle of that battleground. Strangely, and yet powerfully, we are the go-between God and the Devil. We are to submit to God, resist the Devil and all of his workings in order for God to accomplish His will and work on the earth! How amazing is that?

Can you imagine God as the CEO of this world, yet exhorting us to pray for people in areas such as those who are to be hired into the field of harvesting souls? Why doesn't God just send people into the harvest field regardless of man's willingness or unwillingness to pray for the harvest field? Again, the answer is that apparently God has tied Himself to the prayers of mankind over the warfare of the world. We humans He has created are the deciding factor in much of what He does in His spiritual warfare with the Devil.

> But when He saw the multitudes, He was moved with compassion for them, because they were weary and scattered, like sheep having no shepherd. Then He said to His disciples, "The harvest truly is plentiful, but the laborers are few. Therefore pray the Lord of the harvest to send out laborers into His harvest" (Matthew 9:36-38).

It seems as if God wants to answer prayer, yet He cannot do so without the consent of man's prayer and intercession. That's the system that God has set up. He has placed us as coregents in charge of His kingdom. We have a kingdom business relationship with God. From the very beginning when Adam was created in the garden of Eden, God set up the system by which man was to rule over the world that He had created. Man who was made in God's image was to have dominion over all things:

> Then God said, "Let Us make man in our image, according to our likeness; let them have dominion over the fish of the sea, over the birds of the air, and over the cattle, over all the earth and over every creeping thing that creeps on the earth." So God created man in His own image; in the image of God He created him; male

and female He created them. Then God blessed them, and God said to them, "Be fruitful and multiply; fill the earth and subdue it; have dominion over the fish of the sea, over the birds of the air, and over every living thing that moves on the earth" (Genesis 1:26-28).

Not much has changed since then. The Bible says that we were made a little lower than the angels, yet we are in a spiritual warfare over the territory of the world with the very angels who want to conquer the world for the cause of evil and injustice. Victory in this warfare will aid us in helping God in the administration of this world. We are associated with, and participate equally in, a legal contract that God developed for us by His Son Jesus Christ. The Bible says that we are heirs of God because of Christ. This tells us that as God answered the prayers of Jesus, He is sure to answer the prayers of all of His creation as well.

There is a specific task and goal that we have been assigned to complete. There is a mutual cooperation and responsibility to see that our work is accomplished in preparation for the kingdom of God on earth and in heaven. This is an enterprise of "spiritual capital gains" in soul-winning. We share the spiritual profits of bringing people into the kingdom of God. There are five crowns that are mentioned in the Bible that a Christian can receive, and the Soul Winners Crown is one of them. We have been commissioned and authorized to act on His behalf to see that His kingdom grows on the earth before His Son returns to this earth. Then Christ will set in His millennial kingdom. We read statements in the Bible about our work such as:

> All things are of God...and hath given to us the ministry of reconciliation...and hath committed unto us the word of reconciliation (2 Corinthians 5:18-19 KJV).

> As my Father hath sent me, even so send I you (John 20:21 KJV).

> Occupy till I come (Luke 19:13 KJV).

David Siriano

Because of prayer, our part is to be busy for God and to be a witness for the Lord Jesus Christ. It is prayer that prepares us for the work of bringing people into the kingdom of God now, and prepares us to do the business in the kingdom of God that He plans for the future as we reign with Him. We are receiving education, instruction, discipline, and authority in the area of answers to prayer. Answers to prayer are what can convince anyone we talk to about salvation, healing, and the kingdom of God. Prayer helps fill up the kingdom of God on earth today, and grants eternal life to those who become believers. Prayer is on-the-job training for the future kingdom that God has prepared for us, in which we will reign with Him. It says this about our relationship with Christ:

> For thou wast slain, and hast redeemed us to God by thy blood out of every kindred, and tongue, and people, and nation; and hast made us unto our God kings and priests: and we shall reign on the earth (Revelation 5:9-10 KJV).

The future of the kingdom is what God had in mind when He instituted the system of prayer. Not long after prayer was first instituted and the nation of Israel was established, their system of Judaism began to believe in a future messianic kingdom. Prayer and spiritual warfare is the preparation for that divinely appointed kingdom time in the future— through a life that has been heavily influenced by Christ and transformed through Christianity.

Bear in mind that the total restoration and fulfillment of the kingdom is not to take place now as some mistakenly believe. It is not up to the believers to bring a reconstruction of this world before the second coming of Christ. These kinds of changes will not take place until Christ restores the kingdom unto Himself and gains victory over the world. God has given the church a mission on earth to fill His kingdom on earth. We are to win as many souls as possible in order to prepare all of us for this future immeasurable period of time in God's millennial kingdom and in the new heaven and new earth. That brings us to the point of attempting to analyze why God doesn't seem to answer all of our prayers.

WHY DOESN'T GOD ANSWER ALL PRAYERS?

That could be the question of a lifetime. It seems as if God answers some prayers, but He lets others slid by without answers. Sometimes heaven's door seems closed to things that we need or want, or want to accomplish. God may tell us no, or He may say wait a while.

Here's another question. Why are some people healed and others not healed? People with outstanding faith for healing slip into eternity without healing and have to wait until they are instantly healed in the presence of God. I have seen some people with a tremendous amount of faith, far greater than mine and greater than one could ever understand or imagine, yet after they prayed, they were not healed. Many times as a little boy I would attend the healing services of Kathryn Kuhlman. She was a great woman of God who fervently prayed for the sick and inspired tremendous faith in others for healing, yet she said that she didn't know why some people were healed and others were not. Puzzling, isn't it?

There are some people who say that it is God's will that all people should be healed. I believe that statement is true! The apostle John wrote to Gaius in 3 John that his wish was that he would "be in health." That would be a great prayer! However, an equally true statement is that not all people are healed. Why not? Not an easy question to answer. Some people would say that it's a lack of faith. That's a biblical statement to be sure and these situations where someone showed a lack of faith occurred during Jesus' day. The truth of the matter is that not all people are healed for other reasons than a lack of faith. Perhaps they are passing through a situation similar to Job or the apostle Paul when God had to work something out in their lives far beyond even what the greatest preacher or healing evangelist could ever understand or predict.

I believe that another equally true statement according to 1 Timothy 2:4 is that it is God's will that all people should be saved. Again, an equally true statement is that not all people will be saved. Why not? More than likely some people don't believe that it is necessary to trust God for salvation or even believe that He exists. It's just not an important issue in their lives. Again, the truth of the matter is that not all people will be saved because of their rebellion and refusal to believe in God, so therefore they will not go to heaven.

Of course, we know that God expects us to pray and believe Him for answers to the various needs of people. We know and believe that God does things through our fervent prayers. He depends on us. We are managers of His creation with Him and He seems to not be able to do things without our intercession. He wants us to be involved with the spiritual warfare of prayer. So what's the problem?

As previously stated, the biggest mistake we make is to think that spiritual warfare is between us and the Devil. What is happening is that we are only playing out the sidebar demonstrations of warfare here on earth which is just an echo of the powerful warfare that is in the heavens. As already emphasized again and again, the main battle is between God and the Devil, and we are on God's side against the Devil. Their battle won't be won until sometime in the future when God reveals His final authority and victory over the Devil and his counterparts.

What we don't need is the frustration that comes from continual warfare with the Devil as he tries to make it appear that God doesn't answer all of our prayers. It is not our fight. If we are fighting and not trusting God, it may be because the Devil is trying to trick us into believing that God is not there for us and He won't answer our prayers. It is God's fight with the Devil and we need to rest in the fact that God will take care of any battles we may have with the Devil—in His time and for His will and purpose. As it says in James 4:7, "Therefore submit to God. Resist the devil and he will flee from you."

No doubt about it, the Devil wants to prevent individuals from being saved and healed. He does all that he can to prevent those things from happening. If everyone could be saved and if everyone could be healed, there would be no problem with the Devil. If the church could have saved and healed everyone in the past 2,000 years since Christ ascended into heaven then the victory would be ours. Spiritual warfare would have been over a long time ago. The world would have gotten better and there would be no need for the millennial reign of Christ either. We would have won the battle over the Devil and spared the world from the awful tragedies of the future great tribulation.

Theoretically, the Devil would have run back into hell which he deserves, or we could have taken the Devil and cast him into hell. But that's not God's plan. It is God's responsibility, not ours; and it is His plan to totally annihilate the Devil, and He will do so according to His timetable at the end of time. In the meantime, we are holding our ground as defenders of the faith, doing battle against the Devil and his principalities and powers, waiting for the final confrontation between these two archenemies. God is saving the answer to all of our prayers of salvation and healing for the time of the end.

God has given you and me dominion over the earth, to live freely, and to enjoy all of God's creation, to enjoy everything that He has given to us. Even though we wage spiritual warfare in the world, it still belongs to God. We must get this correct if we are going to understand spiritual warfare as well as why not all people are saved and healed. We cannot win the total victory ourselves. God has reserved the final victory of salvation and the victory over sickness and death for all of us who believe in Him solely for Himself. Very few people seem to engage in spiritual warfare so it is up to those who understand it to broaden our knowledge of this warfare and enter into the battle over the world in God's fight with the Devil.

It seems like the battle between these two is on an equal footing and that it is a gigantic toe-to-toe battle that never seems to end. However, the Devil is under the sway and power of Christ, and is only a player in the overall scheme of things. He is a player when it comes to doing his worst deeds against peoples and nations around the world. He has no authority other than what God allows him to have. In fact, the Devil is not even our greatest and final foe. Death is!

My friend, Pastor Dale Andrews of Geneva, New York, gave me some insight about death and the Devil. He reminded me that the apostle Paul told us in 1 Corinthians 15:26 that "The last enemy that will be destroyed is death," not the Devil. He also said that Romans 6:23 doesn't say that the wages of sin is the Devil. It says, "For the wages of sin is death." He said that our greatest enemy is death, not the Devil. I thought that was great insight.

We all know that Jesus said, "I am the resurrection and the life" (John 11:25), which is in total opposition to "death and hell." After all, choosing disobedience and death is what cost us the garden of Eden in the first place. If we give in to the Devil, it's the second death that will keep us out of heaven. We know that Christ died on the cross so that we may be delivered from death and have eternal life. That's the victory. It is not as much victory over the Devil as it is over death!

We know that the Devil is cast into the lake of fire in Revelation 20 at the end time, just like any sinner. He will be tormented in what the Bible calls the "second death." It is after the Devil receives his eternal punishment that the Bible says that "death and hell were cast into the lake of fire." That makes death, along with hell, our final enemy. The Devil doesn't necessarily want us physically dead, he just wants us to worship him and do his will which leads us to spiritual death which is that "second death." Therefore, we don't need to fear the Devil; we need to trust God in faith for the resurrection power over death that He gives to all believers. Victory over death through our salvation and the belief in the resurrection power of Christ is what keeps us from the clutches of the Devil and grants us entrance into heaven. It keeps us from hell and from that "second death." For those of us who have part in the power of Christ's resurrection, that same chapter in the book of Revelation says:

> Blessed and holy is he that hath part in the first resurrection: on such the *second death* hath no power, but they shall be priests of God and of Christ, and shall reign with him a thousand years (Revelation 20:6 KJV).

We are to be in continual warfare in life, victory, and resurrection. We often sing the song that we will "take back what the Devil stole from me." Good statement and a great song! I'm for that. Some who write about spiritual warfare mention taking back the territory that the Devil stole. The Devil tries to discourage us from serving God and robs us of our joy. He brings fear into our lives and robs us of our faith. He puts people in our path who hate us and through them, tries to rob us of our love. Those are just some of the things that the Devil can take from us. What we must do, of course, is hold our ground against the enemy of our soul, and then we can gain great spiritual territorial victories in the areas of salvation and healing, and we must! The church is strong and even hell cannot endure its onslaught and power. As Jesus said to Peter:

On this rock I will build my church, and the gates of Hades shall not prevail against it (Matthew 16:18).

Keep in mind, the territory that the Devil is attempting to take is not just our own personal territory that affects our lives. That territory may be big to us, but it is small in terms of the territory that he is after. While he diverts our attention to focus on our own wants or needs, he goes after God's total territory, which is the entire earth and universe, and the nations and the peoples of the earth so that they will serve him instead of God. He wants them to worship him; his focus is on a far broader territory than what he took from us! Again, the earth is the Lord's, not ours. What the Devil wants is to defeat God and steal the broader territory of worship that belongs to God. Our war with the Devil is over the fact that he wants to turn all of our worship away from God, so that we would live for him and ultimately worship him.

Because America has been founded on godly principles, the Devil is seeking to lead her astray into sin, licentiousness, lawlessness, immorality, perversity, and destruction. He wants us to go beyond the customary or proper boundaries of limits and restraint, disregarding the biblical rules of godliness. He seeks to destroy America by trying to make us believe that we no longer need God. Because of sin, he is possessing people so they will perform deeds of mass murder, killing innocent men, women, and children.

Once sinners are in hell with the Devil, they are more than likely going to abhor him rather than worship him. He deceived them into going to a place where they are far away from the presence of God, being tormented forever and ever. He will probably laugh with ridicule and glee instead of basking in their worship because they will hate him and the place they find themselves in. Don't forget, the Devil will be tormented as well. More than likely he will scornfully deride the sinners as they become the objects of his unsympathetic amusement.

We, in the meantime, are to gain as many victories as we can here and now on earth. It may seem to you that the battle between God and the Devil is at a temporary stalemate until the time of the end. But the battle and the victory is God's. God will bring in total healing and salvation to all who have faith on the earth that believe in Him. We are to take dominion now, but the final dominion is to be taken by Jesus Christ. That takes all that pressure off you and me.

Again, it's not up to us to have the total victory and win the war. That is reserved for God the Father and His Son Jesus Christ. We can win many battles here on earth. Some people are saved, some are healed, and miracles do take place, but the total and final war with its total and final victory over the Devil will be won by God, and not by us. This includes salvations and healings for those who believe.

The truth of the matter is that the world is not getting better; it is getting worse. It has moved far away from bringing glory and honor to God. That's why God will lead the world and the nations of the world into a final onslaught at the battle of Armageddon. Even after that future time, not everyone will be saved and healed. If we could save and heal everyone, it would nullify the need for the book of Revelation, the millennium, and the need for us to see God totally defeat the Devil.

During the time of the millennium, sin itself will not yet be totally eradicated from the earth because Jesus will have to rule the nations with a "rod of iron." The root of sin will still be there in the time of the millennium, but will be subject to Christ's kingdom principles. His kingdom on the earth will dominate the nations.

There are those who may feel that sometimes the Devil is winning and sometimes God is winning, but that's not the truth. The Devil wants us to believe that, but we know that he is a liar. Despite what the Devil accomplishes because of man's disobedience, we know that God triumphs now and in the end because "the battle is the Lord's." Jesus

Christ, when He returns to the earth, will win one hundred percent of the war.

In the final analysis regarding salvation and healing, when Jesus returns to the earth, sets up His heavenly kingdom, creates a new heaven and new earth, and time will be no more, not everyone will be saved and healed. Even God will have to let some people remain unsaved and not healed. He comes to this conclusion:

> He who is unjust, let him be unjust still; he who is filthy, let him be filthy still; he who is righteous, let him be righteous still; he who is holy, let him be holy still (Revelation 22:11).

HOW SATAN GETS A FOOTHOLD

Satan has always tried to dominate men and women through appealing to the flesh. If he could just get his way in our lives, then he can dominate our will and all our actions. The warfare between good and evil is played out in our lives, in our wills, in our hearts, and in what we refer to as the core of our beings. We say that our heart is the expression of our will, our emotions, our love, and what makes us who we are. This is what Satan wants kingship over. If he can rule over our flesh and our will, then he can rule over everything that we do and rule within the principalities and powers. These principalities and powers can play out in our everyday lives and create the dominance that they so eagerly desire in the world. This demonic dominance can apply to our family, our city, our nation, and the world.

This is the root of spiritual warfare in our lives. This is where the godly angels of good can create their influence in our lives, or where we can fall prey to the principalities and powers of evil demonic activity. This is the struggle. This is the warfare, and it starts in us. In a passage of Scripture quoted previously, we can visualize the entry point for the devil taking control of our lives:

David Siriano

> For all that is in the world—the lust of the flesh, the lust of the eyes, and the pride of life—is not of the Father but is of the world. And the world is passing away, and the lust of it; but he who does the will of God abides forever (1 John 2:16-17).

If only the Devil can tempt us to be subservient to the lust that is in our flesh. If only he can appeal to what we see with our eyes. If only he could infatuate us into unwise and unreasonable folly, and cause us to behave foolishly. If only he can affect our pride, so that he can get us to concentrate on what draws us to the world and all of its sin, and take us away from our heavenly Father's will. By giving in to his temptation he has successfully lured us away from the attention we need to give to God. God's will and work then falters because of our sin and disobedience. We are then doing what the devil has tempted us to do and not what God wants us to do. This is the basis of our spiritual warfare.

This warfare centers on whether we will give in to our fleshly desires or rise above them and surrender to God and do His will. Being obedient to God and His will is what will cause eternal life to spring forth in our being and allow us to abide with God forever. The choice becomes what will give us power with God or what will be the power that works within our own will as we give in to temptation. Ephesians 6 perfectly describes this warfare:

> For we do not wrestle against flesh and blood, but against principalities, against powers, against the rulers of the darkness of this age, against spiritual hosts of wickedness in the heavenly places (Ephesians 6:12).

The struggle is immense. The stakes are high. The fight is formidable. The struggle is over souls who will either be brought into the kingdom of God, or souls who will succumb to the treachery and evil of satanic forces. There is a forceful opponent that we are facing. There is an apprehension and dread that should bring us to our knees in prayer. We are instructed in that same chapter, Ephesians 6, to equip ourselves with the spiritual understanding of the immense warfare that engulfs our total being. What we are asked to equip ourselves with is the spiritual armor of God. Notice that putting on the armor of God is for the purpose of spiritual warfare. The putting on of the armor of God immediately follows the statement of our engagement in spiritual warfare:

> Therefore take up the whole armor of God, that you may be able to withstand in the evil day, and having done all, to stand. Stand therefore, having girded your waist with truth, having put on the breastplate of righteousness, and having shod your feet with the preparation of the gospel of peace; above all, taking the shield of faith with which you will be able to quench all the fiery darts of the wicked one. And take the helmet of salvation, and the sword of the Spirit, which is the word of God; praying always with all prayer and supplication in the Spirit, being watchful to this end with all perseverance and supplication for all the saints (Ephesians 6:13-18).

Here is the all-encompassing teaching and analysis of spiritual warfare. This Scripture reveals to us that we are to protect our souls with the spiritual covering of biblical armor that was similar to the armor that was used in physical combat during the apostle Paul's time and in the days of the Old Testament. By faith, we are to take on the life of Jesus Christ Himself. We are to apply to our lives the very things that God has taught us in His Word and everything that we know about the ministry of the Son of God. Spiritual warfare becomes part of our daily living as we fight against the enemy of our souls; and the armor of God is the spiritual strength in our ministry as we serve God.

We are to stand, wearing our spiritual armor as we fight against the Devil himself just as Jesus did during His temptation before the beginning of His ministry. The placement of God's armor to envelop our spiritual being involves truth, righteousness, the gospel of peace, faith, salvation, and the Word of God. These weapons of our spiritual armor are all a part of the warfare against the Devil.

Our waist is the strength of our body, and supports its entire frame. All of our movement is based on the center of our body, carrying the total weight of its parts. So first of all, truth is to be the strength of our spirit and our relationship with God. Without truth in our lives, our entire being is weakened and the testimony of our belief in God becomes a lie. No one will believe what we say without living truthful and honest lives of integrity that are in line with obedience to the Word of God. Without the truth of God's character and the truth of the Son of God within us, our witness of God's salvation can become ineffective.

In physical combat the breastplate of the armor protects the most vulnerable part of the body, the chest. So too, our spiritual breastplate is to be seen as righteousness, or right living before God and this world. The first thing that we want people to see as we face them is the righteousness that we live in; and the only way that we can posses the best possible righteousness is to allow the righteousness of God to live within us.

> But we are all like an unclean thing, and all our
> righteousnesses are like filthy rags (Isaiah 64:6).

Therefore, we must depend on the righteousness of God to fill our lives. When the enemy attacks the very vulnerable part of us and the very core of our being, it is God's righteousness, or our right standing with God, that repels all of the Devil's accusations against us.

Everywhere the souls of our feet take us we are to speak the gospel of the living Word of God. We are to be prepared to speak this gospel of peace to all we come in contact with. While it is true that we are in warfare with the Devil, the gospel is peace, and we must bring peace to the hearer of the gospel. Wherever we walk, we should treat that ground as holy ground and be prepared to talk to anyone who is interested in the gospel. We should always be ready to give an answer to anyone who asks us about our faith, even under the most severe of attacks against us and our testimony.

> *"And do not be afraid of their threats*, nor be troubled."
> But sanctify the Lord God in your hearts, and always

be ready to give a defense to everyone who asks you a
reason for the hope that is in you, with meekness and fear
(1 Peter 3:14-15).

Fighting in combat requires a protective shield that repels any arrow
that will inflict damage on your body. The shield of faith wards off any
attack by the Devil that comes against your soul. Every time an evil
dart flies at you from the enemy of your soul, you can deflect it before
it strikes you.

Wearing a helmet of salvation protects your mind against any
thoughts of wrongdoing against God and any impurity within your own
body and mind. Giving your heart to Christ is one thing, but keeping
your mind on Christ and away from the evil one requires twenty-four
hour per day diligence. The extent that we allow Satan to control our
thoughts and mind is the degree to which he has control over our lives.
Therefore, we are to bring into captivity any thought that is wrong and
submit it to Christ.

For though we walk in the flesh, we do not war according
to the flesh. For the weapons of our warfare are not carnal
but mighty in God for pulling down strongholds, casting
down arguments and every high thing that exalts itself
against the knowledge of God, bringing every thought
into captivity to the obedience of Christ, and being
ready to punish all disobedience when your obedience is
fulfilled (2 Corinthians 10:3-6).

Finally, we are to use what is called the sword of the Spirit, which is
the Word of God. Through the power of the Holy Spirit, we are to take
the Word of God, read it, quote it, and memorize as much of it as we can
in order to use it as a weapon against the enemy.

The warfare that is in the heavens is like two vast armies of angels,
both good and evil, who are trying to influence life here on earth. When
I give in to the influence of evil angels, it gives them the winning edge in
all of my human activity. They have me where they want me. They now
have influence in my life, and I can now influence the lives of others

and the entire world that I am in touch with. They now have the utmost power, both in the world and in the heavenly sphere.

This is where the Devil and the principalities and powers entice us to give in to the lust of the flesh and the eyes so as to distract us from doing God's will. This is where the evil principalities and powers create a positive spin on the sin of pride so that we are lifted up in our own self-gratification. As a result, doing the will of God is of lesser importance, and doing our own will is of greater importance.

This is warfare. This moves us away from doing the work of God. Then the Devil has a greater influence in our lives than God has, and he can dominate our will, our motives, and our life to do his bidding. In multiple situations around the world, in families, villages, towns, cities, and in nations, he can move the pattern of lives in the direction that he dictates; this is how he plans to win the war against God and His people. The struggle in the air is for the control and ownership of the universe, the world, and its people.

By the same token, if I give in to the influence of godly angels in my life, they now have an upper hand in all that I do. Their influence brings me into submission to God. They touch my inner being with godliness and righteousness which they represent. Instead of my mind wandering into evil activity, my mind researches the resourcefulness of God. Similar to Jacob in the Old Testament who wrestled with the angel of God, I too can have authority with the righteous angels and with God, by the godly life that I am attempting to live and by my desire to want more of God's power in my life. Then I can do the work of God and be the hand of God that can influence other people to live for God.

The Bible says that the angels of God minister to those who believe in Him. These angels bring power, protection, and authority in my life. They are sent by God to administer the life that God has given me. They surround me at all times in my life as long as I continue to surrender to God. Their influence in me helps me to create godly influences in the world that I touch. As I minister to others, they are there to support my actions. Praise God for the help they give to our lives. About godly angels, the Bible says:

Intergalactic Warfare

Are they not all ministering spirits, sent forth to minister for them who shall be heirs of salvation? (Hebrews 1:14 KJV)

Chapter Four: Intercessory Prayer

Prayer and intercession are key elements in our relationship with God and with others. Along with fasting they are probably two of the most difficult things that we must do as Christians. Nevertheless they are something that we must continue every day. In Luke 11:1 the disciples of Jesus came to Him and asked Him to teach them to pray. He answered their request by giving them what is commonly known as the Lord's Prayer. It is quoted in that passage in Luke, but it is also found in Matthew 6:

> Our Father which art in heaven, Hallowed be thy name. Thy kingdom come, Thy will be done in earth, as it is in heaven. Give us this day our daily bread. And forgive us our debts, as we forgive our debtors. And lead us not into temptation, but deliver us from evil: For thine is the kingdom, and the power, and the glory, for ever. Amen (Matthew 6:9-13).

That prayer is one of the most well-rounded and all-inclusive prayers that we can offer to God. It establishes the relationship that we have with our heavenly Father, the Creator of the universe. It acknowledges and addresses the fact that we believe in God's will for His kingdom here on earth now and in the future. It asks for daily provision for our needs to be met. It establishes a loving, forgiving, and personal connection that we are to have with others. It deals with the common failures that all of us can face through sin and temptation.

Prayer is defined as personal communication or petition to God, especially by means of adoration, praise, thanksgiving, or supplication for a need. It is our contact with the Supreme Being of the universe who we can worship and who we believe can help us at all times. Prayer can aid us during our times of deepest sorrow and loss. It can bring us through the most difficult times of calamity and personal difficulty. Prayer brings us hope and peace. As we wait on God for answers to our prayers, it can elevate us into the realm of spiritual warfare.

Intercession is the offering of prayers to God on behalf of others. It too can bring us into spiritual warfare as we often pray for others when they sometimes cannot pray for themselves. It can be warfare for their needs or warfare for their souls. It can be warfare with demonic powers that can be life-changing for the individuals we are praying for. It is the connection we make with God for them. It is God's plan to lift us out of our own self-serving prayers and bring us to the place where our mind is on God and on His plan for others. We become challenged to cry out in prayer on behalf of the souls of other people.

Prayer began in the earliest of times and is recorded in the book of Genesis. After the fall of Adam and Eve into sin and after the first recorded murders, people began to call upon God. Abel was murdered by his brother Cain so Eve needed another individual as her seed in this life whom God could work through. Seth was her son who was born to replace the murdered Abel. Look what it says after Seth's son Enos (Enosh) was born:

> And Adam knew his wife again, and she bore a son and named him Seth, "For God has appointed another seed for me instead of Abel, whom Cain killed." And as for Seth, to him also a son was born; and he named him Enosh. Then men began to call on the name of the Lord (Genesis 4:25-26).

In one of Jesus' teachings on prayer, He cited a story of an unjust judge who finally came to the rescue of a widow after she continually begged him for help. This judge didn't fear God or man which meant that he didn't apply any godly principles to his decisions in helping others. He probably showed no mercy or leniency to anyone. Luke 18 tells the story of this widow who continually begged this judge for help in the dire situation that she found herself in. She was being harassed by an adversary of hers. He finally relented to help her because, as the text says, she "troubles me." This showed the great resolve and courage that she had, and is an example for us to be strong in our prayers. In this story, Jesus encouraged His followers to be consistent in prayer:

> Men ought always to pray, and not to faint…shall not God avenge his own elect, which cry day and night unto him, though he bear long with them? I tell you that he will avenge them speedily. Nevertheless when the Son of man cometh, shall he find faith on the earth? (Luke 18:1, 7-8)

Will we as a church continue in prayer and faith until the Lord returns? It is very important that we keep ourselves in a state of constant vigil or watchfulness in prayer through faith. We ourselves must be persistent in our prayers toward God, no matter how long it takes for us to pray through for an answer. Even when it comes to our own personal needs, persistence in our faith is the key. There are several examples in the Bible that reflect great faith on the part of the seekers who wanted to believe for healing. A few of those examples in the New Testament were:

1. The Roman centurion who in Matthew 8:5-13 had a servant who was ill, but the centurion did not want Jesus to even enter his home because he felt unworthy; he simply asked Jesus to speak the word and his servant would be healed. Jesus said, "I have not found such great faith, not even in Israel." His servant was healed.

2. Blind Bartimaeus in Mark 10:46-52 continually cried for Jesus to have mercy on him. Because of his persistence in faith, Jesus called him out of the crowd and healed him.

3. A paralyzed man in Luke 5:18-26 was let down through the roof of a house on a cot by his friends because Jesus was there with a large crowd and they couldn't get in. When Jesus saw their faith, He healed the man and forgave his sins.

4. The woman with a severe blood disease in Luke 8:43-48 simply touched the hem of Jesus' garment in the press of the crowd, and she was healed immediately. Jesus felt virtue or strength and power leave His body because of the faith of that woman.

Adding to the faith that we are supposed to have, even the Holy Spirit gets involved in our prayers. Romans 8 speaks about all of creation that is in a state of constant mournfulness to be set free from the bondage of corruption and vanity that it finds itself in. Creation has the hope and expectation of deliverance from this life to a life of liberty when it is free from the bonds of this earth. Paul then mentions that the Holy Spirit can help us in the prayers that we make when we are in a state of weakness. When we are emotionally, physically, or spiritually weak, I believe that the Holy Spirit can help us when persistence in prayer is needed. A Scripture mentioned earlier says:

> Likewise the Spirit also helps in our weaknesses. For we do not know what we should pray for as we ought, but the Spirit Himself makes intercession for us with groanings which cannot be uttered. Now He who searches the hearts knows what the mind of the Spirit is, because He makes intercession for the saints according to the will of God (Romans 8:26-27).

Notice that the Holy Spirit knows how to pray for us according to the will of God. He knows what is best for us. He knows whether or not we are praying with selfishness. Therefore, sometimes God's answer to us is yes, sometimes it is no, and sometimes it is wait until you are mature enough in order to receive the answer and apply it to your life correctly and without selfishness. That passage in Romans 8 goes on to say this:

> And we know that all things work together for good to them that love God, to them who are the called according to his purpose (Romans 8:28 KJV).

The Holy Spirit was sent to the earth after Jesus Christ came to be the ultimate sacrifice for man's sin. After many years of continual sacrificial offerings by the Jews through the system of Judaism, it was God in the form of Jesus Christ who came to earth to rescue people from their sin. He came to God's chosen people, the nation of Israel.

After His years of ministry on the earth, His sacrifice on the cross of Calvary in Jerusalem, and after His ascension to heaven, Jesus sent the Holy Spirit to continue His ministry on the earth through the church. The power of the Holy Spirit is at work in the world today. The Holy Spirit is carrying on God's work in the midst of the spiritual warfare that is prevalent throughout the world.

> Nevertheless I tell you the truth. It is to your advantage that I go away; for if I do not go away, the Helper will not come to you; but if I depart, I will send Him to you. And when He has come, He will convict the world of *sin*, and of *righteousness*, and of *judgment*: of sin, because they do not believe in Me; of righteousness, because I go to My Father and you see Me no more; of judgment, because the ruler of this world is judged (John 16:7-11).

This is the reason we must become involved in intercessory prayer because this Scripture shows the three things that the Holy Spirit has come to the earth to do in this massive battle with the evils of this world. He has come to convince or overwhelm in argument the three things that the people of this world do not want to talk about: sin, righteousness, and judgment. The problem is that anyone in the world who is not interested in confessing Christ does not want to hear any reproof from the Holy Spirit.

Sometimes those we attempt to witness to do not want to hear that, first of all, they are sinners and they need to believe in Jesus Christ. Second, they do not want to hear that in order to get to heaven they need to walk in righteousness and holiness. Because Jesus Christ has gone to heaven, God's righteousness must now be seen in the church. Third, they certainly do not want to hear that someday they will stand before the Judge of the whole world and be judged for their sins. That passage in John says that the Devil is judged already so, of course, those who follow him will be judged too.

I believe that it is this restraining power of the Holy Spirit that keeps the evil of this world in check. The Holy Spirit is at work within the church, and He is here to complete the work that Jesus Christ was sent to do. Jesus said, "As my Father hath sent me, even so send I you" (John 20:21 KJV). One day this powerful restraining Spirit will be removed as the church is "caught up" into heaven before the great tribulation. For now, He is holding back the power of the spiritual enemy. I believe that 2 Thessalonians is talking about the Holy Spirit who is active within the church of Jesus Christ:

> Do you not remember that when I was still with you I told you these things? And now you know what is restraining, that he may be revealed in his own time. For the mystery of lawlessness is already at work; only He who now restrains will do so until He is taken out of the way (2 Thessalonians 2:5-7).

This restraining power of the Holy Spirit is at work within us. That is why, when it comes to intercession for others, we must participate in this every day through the power of the Holy Spirit as we inquire of God's mind as to how to pray for others. We must lift ourselves out of the self-centeredness that we usually live in and think of others and pray for them. There are others who many times cannot have the faith that is needed, so we must pray for them that they find that faith so that their needs can be met. God will use us in prayer if we let Him and if we surrender our prayer life to His will. We can help gain the victory for ourselves and for others.

We must not give up on our prayer for others. This spiritual warfare between God and the Devil involves every ounce of strength that we can muster as we join in this fight. Faith and continuance in prayer are the keys. Even though the world is going in the wrong direction, we must remember that Christ is the ultimate victor in the battle of the ages. We must continue in our struggle of spiritual warfare because it is something that we will be involved in for the rest of our lives. We must remember that Christ is the ultimate and eventual victor.

> In the world ye shall have tribulation: but be of good cheer; I have overcome the world (John 16:33 KJV).

Intercession involves perseverance on our part to believe that an answer will come from God on behalf of the others we are praying for. It requires steadfastness until an answer comes. It involves seeking, asking, and entreating God, or beseeching and imploring Him for an answer for them, no matter what that answer is. It is a prayer that we pray for in the Spirit and a petition of prayer for others that is revealed by Paul:

> Praying always with all prayer and supplication in the Spirit, and watching thereunto with all perseverance and supplication for all saints (Ephesians 6:18 KJV).

PRINCIPLES FOR EFFECTIVE INTERCESSION

Following are ten "Principles for Effective Intercession" written by Joy Dawson in 1985 that still speak to us today. These are principles of intercession that we should put into practice every day of our lives. They are reprinted with permission.

1. **Praise God for who He is, and for the privilege of engaging in the same wonderful ministry as the Lord Jesus.**

   "He always lives to make intercession for them (His own)*"* (Hebrews 7:25).

   Praise God for the privilege of cooperating with Him in the affairs of men through prayer.

2. **Make sure your heart is clean before God, by having given the Holy Spirit time to convict, should there be any unconfessed sin.**

   "If I regard iniquity in my heart, the Lord will not hear" (Psalms 66:18).

Intergalactic Warfare

"Search me, O God, and know my heart; try me, and know my anxieties; and see if there is any wicked way in me, and lead me in the way everlasting" (Psalms 139:23-24).

Check carefully in relation to resentment to anyone. Notice the link between forgiveness and prayer in God's Word.

When Jesus instructs the disciples how to pray He says, *"Forgive us our debts, as we forgive our debtors"* (Matthew 6:12). *Immediately following* the Lord's Prayer He says, *"For if you forgive men their trespasses, your Heavenly Gather will also forgive you. But if you do not forgive men their trespasses, neither will your Father forgive your trespasses"* (Matthew 6:14-15).

"And whenever you stand praying, if you have anything against anyone, forgive him, that your Father in heaven may also forgive you your trespasses" (Mark 11:25).

Now notice the link between forgiveness and faith when we pray.

"Whatever things you ask when you pray, believe that you receive them, and you will have them" (Mark 11:24).

" 'Take heed to yourselves. If your brother sins against you, rebuke him; and if he repents, forgive him. And if he sins against you seven times in a day, and seven times in a day returns to you, saying, "I repent," you shall forgive him.' And the apostles said to the Lord, 'Increase our faith.' So the Lord said, 'If you have faith as a mustard seed, you can say to this mulberry tree, "Be pulled up by the roots and be planted in the sea," and it would obey you' " (Luke 17:3-6).

Job had to forgive his friends for their wrong judging of him, before he could pray effectively for them.

"And the Lord restored Job's losses when he prayed for his friends. Indeed, the Lord gave Job twice as much as he had before" (Job 42:10).

"Faith which worketh by love" (Galatians 5:6 KJV).

3. **Acknowledge you can't really pray without the direction and energy of the Holy Spirit.**

   "The Spirit also helps in our weaknesses. For we do not what we should pray for as we ought" (Romans 8:26).

Ask God to utterly control you by His Spirit, receive by faith that He does, and thank Him.

   "Be filled with the Spirit" (Ephesians 5:18).

   "Without faith it is impossible to please Him" (Hebrews 11:6).

4. **Deal aggressively with the enemy. Come against him in the all-powerful name of the Lord Jesus Christ and with the "sword of the Spirit," the Word of God.**

   "Therefore submit to God. Resist the devil and he will flee from you" (James 4:7).

5. **Die to your own imaginations, desires, and burdens for what you feel you should pray.**

   "Lean not unto thine own understanding" (Proverbs 3:5-6 KJV).

   "He who trusts in his own heart is a fool" (Proverbs 28:26).

   "My thoughts are not your thoughts" (Isaiah 55:8).

6. **Praise God now in faith for the remarkable prayer meeting you're going to have. He's a remarkable God and will do something consistent with His character.**

7. **Wait before God in silent expectancy, listening for His direction.**

    "My soul, wait silently for God alone, for my expectation is from Him" (Psalms 62:5).

    "Therefore I will look to the Lord; I will wait for the God of my salvation; my God will hear me" (Micah 7:7).

    "But My people would not heed My voice, and Israel would have none of Me. So I gave them over to their own stubborn heart, to walk in their own counsels. Oh, that My people would listen to Me, that Israel would walk in My ways!" (Psalms 81:11-13).

8. **In obedience and faith, utter what God brings to your mind, believing.**

    "My sheep hear My voice...and they follow Me" (John 10:27).

    Keep asking God for direction, expecting Him to give it to you. He will.

    "I will instruct you and teach you the way you should go; I will guide you with My eye" (Psalms 32:8).

    Make sure you don't move on to the next subject until you've given God time to discharge all He wants to say to you regarding this particular burden, especially when praying in a group.

    Be encouraged from the lives of Moses, Daniel, Paul, and Anna, that God gives revelation to those who make intercession a way of life.

9. **If possible have your Bible with you should God want to give you direction or confirmation from it.** *"Your word is a lamp to my feet and a light to my path"* (Psalms 119:105).

10. **When God ceases to bring things to your mind to pray for, finish by praising and thanking Him for what He has done, reminding yourself of Romans 11:36, "For of Him and through Him and to Him are all things, to whom be glory forever. Amen."**[7]

A WARNING

God knows the weakness of the human heart toward pride, and if we speak of what God has revealed and done in intercession, it may lead to committing this sin.

God shares His secrets with those who are able to keep them.

There may come a time when He definitely prompts us to share, but unless this happens we should remain silent.

> *But they kept quiet, and told no one in those days any of the things they had seen* (Luke 9:36).

> *But Mary kept all these things and pondered them in her heart* (Luke 2:19).

Prayer has been encouraged throughout the Bible and we see marvelous instances in which prayers were answered. Many times the people of God were discouraged or reached a point of desperation, but God always came through for them. The Bible goes on to tell us that we should always pray and not faint or lose hope, because time and time again, God's hand has moved on behalf of His people. Successful prayers are found throughout the pages of Scripture. God was always there for His people in instances such as when:

1. Moses cried to the Lord when there was no water and cast a tree into bitter waters for the children of Israel to drink, and the waters were made sweet.

---

7. Joy Dawson, Principles for Effective Intercession. Copyright 1985. Reprinted with permission.

2. Gideon prayed for extra assurance from God that Israel would be victorious in battle by placing a fleece of wool on the ground for it to be damp during one night and dry on another night as a sign.

3. Hannah prayed for a child when she was barren of children, and Samuel was born to her who later became a great prophet in Israel.

4. King Solomon prayed for the house of God that he built, that it would be hallowed unto God.

5. The Prophet Elijah prayed for fire to fall from heaven on the sacrifice that he made to prove that Jehovah, the God of Israel, was the true God when he challenged the false prophets of the god, Baal.

6. Zachariah prayed for a child to be born of his wife, Elizabeth, who was barren; and she gave birth to a son who became John the Baptist.

Many of these well-known or notable prayers have been prayed that created a mighty impact for the one praying and for others. The following prayers moved the hand of God when it came to salvation, deliverance, and strength for God's people.

1. Abraham prayed for Sodom even though he knew that very few righteous people were living there. His nephew, Lot, was saved from its destruction.

2. Ezra prayed for the sins of the captive children of Israel when they were in Babylon. His prayers got them back on course.

3. The prayer of our Lord Jesus Christ is recorded in John 17, and reflects His attitude in prayer for Himself, His disciples, and for others in the world.

Answers to prayer for one's self and intercessory prayer for others have the assurance that God will answer. In fact, encouragement to pray comes not only from God but from His prophets and apostles. There are some wonderful promises that are found in God's Word. Believe these promises for your life and for those you pray for:

He shall call upon Me, and I will answer him; I *will* be with him in trouble; I will deliver him and honor him (Psalms 91:15).

And it shall come to pass that before they call, I will answer; and while they are still speaking, I will hear (Isaiah 65:24).

So I say to you, ask, and it will be given to you; seek, and you will find; knock, and it will be opened to you (Luke 11:9).

If you abide in Me, and My words abide in you, you will ask what you desire, and it shall be done for you (John 15:7).

WAYS TO PRAY FOR PEOPLE IN AUTHORITY

In our times of intercession we need to see the importance of praying for our leaders. Political leaders have much to do with the success or failure of any nation; therefore it is of crucial importance to pray for them. It is their spiritual understanding and personal obedience to God that makes them effective leaders. Therefore that makes it critical for us to pray for them. The Bible makes this crystal clear. We need to know how to pray and what to pray for.

Therefore I exhort first of all that supplications, prayers, intercessions, and giving of thanks be made for all men, for kings and all who are in authority, that we may lead a quiet and peaceable life in all godliness and reverence. For this is good and acceptable in the sight of God our Savior, who desires all men to be saved and to come to the knowledge of the truth (1 Timothy 2:1-4).

I'd like to share the following "30 Ways to Pray for People in Authority" by Gary P. Bergel.

The life of every citizen of every nation is impacted by a vast multitude of individuals who wield significant influence each day.

Intergalactic Warfare

Consider: millions of elected officials, appointed judges, lawyers, police officers, bureaucrats, military officers, business executives and managers, those involved in church leadership, educators, medical practitioners, and hospital administrators.

How might we pray for these individuals? Here are thirty things based on Scripture that we can pray for people in authority. Don't overwhelm yourself. Select one person or group of people and then pray one of these things each day for them.

1. That they be God fearing and recognize that they are accountable to Him for each decision and act (Proverbs 9:10).

2. That they be granted wisdom, knowledge, and understanding (James 1:5).

3. That they be presented with the gospel and a loving Christian witness (Romans 10:14).

4. That, if unsaved, they be drawn to a saving encounter with Christ; if born-again, they be strengthened and encouraged in their faith (1 Timothy 2:4; Ephesians 1:17-23).

5. That they recognize their own inadequacy and pray and seek the will of God (Proverbs 3:5-8; Luke 11:9-13).

6. That they be convicted of sin, transgression, and iniquity (Psalms 51:17; John 8:9).

7. That they heed their conscience, confess their sins, and repent (Proverbs 28:13; James 4:8).

8. That they read the Bible and attend prayer meetings and Bible studies (Psalms 119:11; Colossians 3:2).

9. That they value and regard the Ten Commandments and the teachings of Christ (Psalms 19:7-11; John 8:31-32).

10. That they respect and honor their own parents if living (Ephesians 6:2-3).

11. That they respect authority and practice accountability (Romans 13:1-7).

12. That they be given godly counsel and God-fearing advisors (Proverbs 24:6).

13. That they be honest and faithful to spouses and children (Malachi 2:15-16).

14. That they be practicing members of local congregations (Hebrews 10:25).

15. That they desire purity and avoid debauchery, pornography, perversion, and drunkenness (1 Corinthians 6:9-20; Titus 2:12).

16. That they be timely, reliable, and dependable (Matthew 21:28-31).

17. That they be honest in financial, tax, and also ethical matters (1 Corinthians 6:10; 1 Timothy 6:6-10).

18. That they seek pastoral care and counsel when needed (Hebrews 13:7).

19. That they seek out and nurture godly friendships (Psalms 1:1-3).

20. That they have thankful and teachable spirits (Romans 1:21).

21. That they be generous and have compassionate hearts for the poor and needy (Psalms 112:9; Luke 10:33-37).

22. That they redeem their time and know priorities (Ephesians 5:15-17).

23. That they desire honesty, integrity, and loyalty (Psalms 26; Proverbs 11:3).

24. That they have courage to resist manipulation, pressure, and the fear of man (Proverbs 29:25; 2 Timothy 1:7).

25. That they be shielded from occultism, New Age cults, false religions, and secret societies (Isaiah 1:29; 2:6).

26. That they be presented with biblical worldviews and principles (Ephesians 3:10).

27. That they endeavor to restore the sanctity of life, families, divine order, and morality in our nation (Ephesians 5:22-6:4).

28. That they would work to reverse the trends of humanism in our nation (1 Chronicles 12:32; Isaiah 59:19).

29. That they desire humility and meekness and be willing to serve and cooperate (John 13:14; Titus 3:1-2).

30. That they be prepared to give account to Almighty God (Hebrews 9:27).[8]

It is as we pray using all of these principles suggested in this chapter that we will see day by day victory through Christ for ourselves and those we pray for. Prayer changes things. It is what can turn certain loss, ruin, and disaster into successful living in the Spirit. God is the one who answers prayer, and He is the one who is there to hear us as we intercede for our families, our spiritual leaders, and the leaders in our nation. Remember praying for ourselves and interceding for others, including our leaders, is helping God win the day by day spiritual warfare with the Devil.

---

8. Gary Bergel, *30 Ways to Pray for All in Authority*, 2002, first published by Intercessors for America, www.ifapray.org, Reprinted with permission.

Chapter Five: Why Nations Go To War

WHERE HAS GOD BEEN?

Why have there been so many wars throughout the history of the world? Why has man been in so much conflict with his neighbor, or why have there been so many nations that have risen in hatred and violence with their neighboring nations? Where has God been while so much conflict has troubled the world? Why does God allow all the wars to continue to engulf our world, and does that mean that God approves of the violence?

It seems as if God has turned a deaf ear to the violence and terrorism that has rocked our world. It seems that He has turned His back on the people He has created and has loved. There are some who view God as an uninterested Creator who has spun His creation out into a vast universe and taken His hands off of the world He has created. This is the view of those called Deists. As already mentioned, they view God as someone who has let the world wallow in its own conflict and turmoil, trying to figure out its own destiny. Is that true? Has God left us alone? Can we expect more from a God who not only created the world, but sent His own divinity to the world in the form of His Son, Jesus Christ?

Certainly, the Bible as a book of history records not only the people of the world as a family, with beautiful, rich, and compelling stories of love and compassion, but it also records a created people, filled with violence and hatred. The Bible not only records much of the ancient wars and conflicts of the world, it also records the words of Jesus that propel His thoughts to a time of the future where there would be war and violence like never before. His words were spoken nearly 2,000 years ago during the height of the Roman Empire, but graphically describe a time in the future.

In light of the centuries of conflict from the time of Jesus until the twenty-first century, His words ring out a deafening sound that can only trigger an alarm in the human heart that terrorism and violence will only get worse as time unfolds. Man has lived in sin and continues to live in sin. The reason God allows so much war is because man has refused to listen to God and has turned away from His outstretched hand. Nations continue to try to dominate each other because of that sin. Jesus said about the end times:

> And you will hear of wars and rumors of wars. See that you are not troubled; for all these things must come to pass, but the end is not yet. For nation will rise against nation, and kingdom against kingdom (Matthew 24:6-7).

When Jesus spoke those words, there had been a countless number of wars before His time, and there have been a countless number of wars since His time. It seems as if war is part of the fabric of life itself. It certainly is a part of the fabric of the nations. God has not left us alone. It's just that war is clearly a sign of man's sin and thus the world's desperation; it is also a part of the end times we live in.

The wars of this world are a part of the clash that involves the spiritual warfare that has been going on ever since Satan fell into sin and was thrown out of the throne room of God. Satan has taken this warfare to individual lives and to the nations of the world. He has tried to control the nations, but the best he has been able to do is to try to disrupt God's plan which leads to the end times. Despite the wars, God is the one who is in charge of this world and we have nothing to fear.

GOD IS IN CONTROL OF THE WORLD

There has been so much war and conflict in the world because of man's sin. Man has seldom tried to obey a loving, compelling, and merciful God. I'm sure that God watches the trouble in this world with dismay. He doesn't approve of violence, but He allows it to take place. As the ultimate power in the universe, all other powers involving the "principalities and powers, the rulers of darkness, and the spiritual wickedness in high places" are under His control. This also includes the Devil. God in the form of Jesus Christ has all this power as well. As previously quoted, God the Father:

> Raised Him from the dead and seated Him at His right hand in the heavenly places, far above all principality and power and might and dominion, and every name that is named, not only in this age but also in that which is to come. And He put all things under His feet, and gave Him to be head over all things to the church, which is His body, the fullness of Him who fills all in all (Ephesians 1:20-23).

God's has a master plan that will bring about the annihilation of His enemies and the enemies of man during one final conflict and show of power during the battle of Armageddon. God has not left us alone. He is in control of all the world's powers. The nations of the world are birthed at His command. As previously stated in Acts 17:26, it is God who determines the appointed times and the boundaries of the dwellings of the nations. He is the one who says when the nations come to power and when their power ends. It is God who sets up their boundaries. It is not the Devil who is in charge of their times of existence and their boundaries, but God.

> He makes nations great, and destroys them; He enlarges nations, and guides them (Job 12:23).

What is even more disconcerting for those who are God's enemies is that God has the ability to know the beginning of things up until the time they finally conclude. He can predict the future because He knows what the future holds. He knows the beginning of time from the end of time. That gives Him the advantage of formulating a master plan that only He can devise and only He can implement to His liking. It says that very thing in Isaiah:

> Remember the former things of old, for I am God, and
> there is no other; I am God, and there is none like Me,
> *declaring the end from the beginning*, and from ancient
> times things that are not yet done, saying, "My counsel
> shall stand, and I will do all My pleasure" (Isaiah 46:9-10).

How can we, as finite people, understand an infinite God? How can we even come close to knowing God's plan? We realize that God is much more brilliant than we are, and that when He speaks, things get accomplished according to what He desires.

> "For My thoughts are not your thoughts, nor are your
> ways My ways," says the Lord. For as the heavens are
> higher than the earth, so are My ways higher than your
> ways, and My thoughts than your thoughts. For as the
> rain comes down, and the snow from heaven, and do
> not return there, but water the earth, and make it bring
> forth and bud, that it may give seed to the sower and
> bread to the eater, so shall My word be that goes forth
> from My mouth; it shall not return to Me void, but it
> shall accomplish what I please, and it shall prosper in the
> thing for which I sent it" (Isaiah 55:8-11).

The best that we can do to understand God's thoughts and His mighty plan for the nations of the world is to try and understand God's way of dealing with nations in the past. Simply put, *if you want to know what God is going to do in the future, you must find out what He's done in the past.* That will give you an indication of His plans.

God has a way of dealing with nations and He is consistent. As nations are embroiled in spiritual warfare, God doesn't change His methods. What He has done 1,000 years ago or 3,000 years ago, He still does today.

Another thing to remember is that *God uses both good and evil to accomplish His desire and will for the world.* As an example, in the Bible God has used lying prophets, prostitutes, and evil kings to accomplish His will. In more modern times, God used both the good empires such as the United States and England, and an evil empire such as the USSR to crush the evil dictator, Adolf Hitler, during World War II when Hitler was killing millions of Jews. That war, along with World War I, helped bring the Jews back to their land in the twentieth century. That was one of the reasons God allowed the establishment of the United States as a superpower.

God knows just how to use these empires and how far to allow them to go with their power. God will let them continue in evil for just so long a period of time before He steps in to curtail or restrain their ways. In the end, the master plan of God will have its way. God will receive all of the glory. Even if man does not praise Him, his evil works will praise Him. The Bible declares that the wrath of man will bring glory to God and the rest of the wrath of man, God will keep under His control.

> Surely the wrath of man shall praise thee: the remainder of wrath shalt thou restrain (Psalms 76:10 KJV).

God has used nations against each other as punishment for their sin. Because of the spiritual warfare between God and the Devil over control of the nations, this warfare has been played out on the worldly nations who do battle with each other. Demonic spirits have tried to dominate the nations and have clashed with godly spirits. Even when these godless nations have tried to dominate God's chosen nation, Israel, spirits have clashed over who would maintain control over Israel. When God sent godless nations to fight against His people because of their disobedience, God would then punish these invading nations because of their pride, injustice, and immorality and their dominance over His chosen people.

The wars that have been carried out over the centuries are a reflection of the warfare between the godly principalities and the evil principalities in the heavens. Simply put, the spiritual powers in the heavens are warring with each other for control of the nations of the world and the people who reside in those nations. Their battles in the heavens are being played out in the battles on the earth. The godly powers are interested in allowing a free flow of the gospel and an understanding of God while the evil powers are interested in bringing the peoples of the nations into rebellion, war, and murder. The evil political leaders think that they are in control instead of God. The godly powers want the nations to serve the Lord and proclaim that God helps them, while the evil powers bring the nations under the power and sway of the Devil with little or no regard for God's help.

Vying for territories and the peoples of those territories is the primary focus of both good and evil powers. Sometimes independence and fighting for freedoms are of important interest in the cause of godliness and fairness to man, while keeping man under subjection would be the goal of evil powers. Therefore evil fights against man's freedom. Occasionally these two goals become intertwined and confusing, so that sometimes it is difficult to know the difference between a righteous action of war and an unrighteous action of war.

At the center of all these wars is a claim by the book of Genesis about a plan that God instituted a long time ago, long before any other plans of nationalism were made by man. It is a plan that will culminate in the book of Revelation. It is a plan that involves the sons of Isaac and the sons of Ishmael. It involves promises that were carried out in the lives of the Jews and the lives of the Arab people. Both of their histories have roots in the Middle East and their current desire for position and authority is the land of Canaan, otherwise known as Palestine. They both lay claim to the temple mount area, and want the freedom to practice their faith and to lead their lives as they want. Both of these peoples are also rooted in the book of Genesis as they fight to retain their possession of the land of Israel and as they both attempt to maintain control of the temple area. God is the only one who can settle their differences and He will do so when He sends His Son Jesus Christ to return to the earth again. This will happen at the end of the great tribulation during the battle of Armageddon.

THE LAND OF CANAAN (PALESTINE)

What are God's thoughts for the nation of Israel and how are they involved in spiritual warfare? What ways has He planned out for them? What has been God's Word for His chosen people since the time of the book of Genesis? Has God changed His mind regarding the early promises He made to them? Has He changed His mind about the promises that were made to the Arab people who occupy most of the Middle East? This is what He says to Abraham:

> I will make you a great nation; I will bless you and make your name great; and you shall be a blessing. I will bless those who bless you, and I will curse him who curses you; and in you all the families of the earth shall be blessed (Genesis 12:2-3).

Abraham had two sons. He had Ishmael with Hagar, Sarah's handmaid, because Sarah did not bear any children, and then he had Isaac with Sarah in her older years. At first glance the above Scripture could appear that this primary blessing could fall upon either one of Abraham's children. However, a closer look at Scripture reveals other statements of blessing from God that indicate that the birthright blessing, or double portion blessing belonged to Isaac. This would include the everlasting covenant of the land of Canaan, and the blessing that would bring the coming of the Messiah.

After God's blessing was pronounced to be on Isaac who was soon to be born to Sarah, and not on his firstborn Ishmael, Abraham begged God for a blessing on Ishmael as well. Both sons received a blessing from God. We read in Genesis 17 that the primary blessing that was bestowed upon Abraham was passed on to Isaac. It mentions the blessing given to Isaac quite clearly:

> I will make you exceedingly fruitful; and I will make nations of you, and kings shall come from you. And I will establish My covenant between Me and you and your descendants after you in their generations, for an everlasting covenant, to be God to you and your descendants after you. Also I give to you and your descendants after you the land in which you are a stranger, all the land of Canaan, as an everlasting possession; and I will be their God (Genesis 17:6-8).

Intergalactic Warfare

Then God said to Abraham, "As for Sarai your wife, you shall not call her name Sarai, but Sarah shall be her name. And I will bless her and also give you a son by her; then I will bless her, and she shall be a mother of nations; kings of peoples shall be from her" (Genesis 17:15-16).

And Abraham said to God, "Oh, that Ishmael might live before You!" Then God said: "No, Sarah your wife shall bear you a son, and you shall call his name Isaac; I will establish My covenant with him for an everlasting covenant, and with his descendants after him" (Genesis 17:18-19).

In the verses that follow in that same chapter, we discover that God had a blessing for Ishmael as well (Genesis 21:12-21). The sons of Ishmael would occupy much territory. Nations and lands would belong to him as his children and his children's children would spread throughout the Middle East, forming the great Arab peoples of the Middle East. However, the primary blessing belonged to Isaac.

This blessing to Isaac was an everlasting, enduring, and unconditional covenant. Therefore, those who bless Israel will be blessed and those who curse Israel will be cursed. This blessing to Isaac even included the land of Canaan, which belonged to him and his offspring and not to Ishmael. That's the way it was throughout the days of the Bible and that's the controversy that is problematic today, but the Bible supports Isaac's family occupying that land.

God gave the sons of Isaac a certain land grant and God gave the sons of Ishmael a certain land grant. God gave Israel access and right to the land of Canaan. Ishmael settled on land that was surrounding all the land of Canaan. Ishmael had twelve sons who became the founders of the Ishmaelite tribes who went on to occupy the territories from Egypt to modern day Iraq and beyond. They had rights to most of these lands that were given to them by God through the promise made to them in Genesis. I have to believe that if the sons of Ishmael have rights to their land then the sons of Isaac have the rights to the land of Canaan.

The Promised Land provided to Abraham to be passed on to his son Isaac was the land identified in Genesis 15:18-21. This land is described as being situated from the river of Egypt known as the Nile River, north to the great river called the Euphrates River. This pretty much encompasses all of the land of Palestine today, and then some. During the time of King David's and King Solomon's kingdoms when Israel was at its most powerful time in antiquity, this was the maximum extent of the land that was given to the nation of Israel.

Further descriptions of the land given to Isaac are found elsewhere in the Bible. We see precise borders given in Exodus 23:31 that mention the Red Sea, the Sea of the Philistines (the Mediterranean), and the river which is the river Euphrates. Other Scriptures that give various boundaries are 1 Kings 4:21, 24 and 2 Chronicles 9:26. The land that was given to the twelve tribes of Israel through Moses is mentioned in Numbers 34:1-15, and the land that seems to be yet for a future time, when Israel will rule during the millennium is found in Ezekiel 47:13-20.

In the Bible, Abraham was given separate blessings for himself and his family; they are found in Genesis chapters 12-17. One blessing was for the descendants of his son Isaac, found in Genesis 17:1-8 and in Deuteronomy 1:7-8. The other blessing was for the descendants of Ishmael, found in Genesis 16:11-13; 17:20; 21:9-21. In this second covenant that was given to Ishmael, the Lord promised to make his descendants one great nation (Genesis 17:20; 21:13, 18), and that his descendants would live in hostility with all men. Just before Ishmael was born, the Lord spoke to Hagar his mother these telling words:

> And the Angel of the Lord said to her: "Behold, you are with child, and you shall bear a son. You shall call his name Ishmael, because the Lord has heard your affliction. *He shall be a wild man; his hand shall be against every man, and every man's hand against him.* And he shall dwell in the presence of all his brethren" (Genesis 16:11-12).

This is a scenario that is being carried out even to this day. The division and warfare between the sons of Isaac being God's chosen ones to dwell in Palestine and the sons of Ishmael being God's chosen to dwell in much of the Middle East is part of the massive spiritual warfare that is going on in the heavens even today. Both of these powerful people with roots in the book of Genesis are part of the world's struggle, as they disagree over the fundamental area of Jerusalem. The Devil wants to thwart the plan for Israel in the last days by bringing the Arab world upon them. He wants to interrupt the plan of God in the end times so that the nation of Israel will not enter the millennial time with Christ as ruler as Scripture predicts.

This is where you and I fit into the picture in regard to spiritual warfare and the Middle East. Our prayer in warfare should be that God would preserve the nation of Israel as an intact nation for the Jews. Our prayer should be that God would bring as much peace as possible to that area. The reason is that in the future during the time of the great tribulation, the Devil will pounce down upon the Middle East and will try to prevent the nation of Israel from maintaining their land. Peace will be difficult to maintain.

Today, a possible plan for the land of Israel is that it may be given over to a two-state solution. Perhaps the Jews will occupy their portion of Palestine and the Arab people living in Palestine will occupy their portion of Palestine. That is not the biblical solution, but I believe that will be man's solution. I predict the possibility that there will be a deal that will try to appease all parties. It will be a politics for land, for temple, for nation deal, that will be brokered. The Jews will get their temple and the Arab peoples will get their land and the state that they desperately want. Peace will be a tentative solution until the battle of Armageddon. An eerie prediction is made about the children of Israel and the nations of the world who will gather together for battle in the last days.

> "The Lord will roar from on high, and utter His voice from His holy habitation; He will roar mightily against His fold. He will give a shout, as those who tread the grapes, against all the inhabitants of the earth. A noise will come to the ends of the earth—for *the Lord has a controversy with the nations*; He will plead His case with all flesh.

He will give those who are wicked to the sword," says the Lord. Thus says the Lord of hosts: "Behold, disaster shall go forth from nation to nation, and a great whirlwind shall be raised up from the farthest parts of the earth. And at that day the slain of the Lord shall be from one end of the earth even to the other end of the earth. They shall not be lamented, or gathered, or buried; they shall become refuse on the ground" (Jeremiah 25:30-33).

For behold, *in those days and at that time, when I bring back the captives of Judah and Jerusalem, I will also gather all nations*, and bring them down to the Valley of Jehoshaphat; and *I will enter into judgment with them* there *on account of My people, My heritage Israel, whom they have scattered among the nations; they have also divided up My land* (Joel 3:1-2).

In the realm of spiritual warfare, the evil principalities will be the aggressors. They will maintain power during the great tribulation until the battle of Armageddon happens that will resolve the issue when Christ returns to the world. He will return victorious. He will destroy those principalities and powers that have been so prevalent up to and until that time. It will be a warfare between church and state as Christ, representing Christianity, battles against the nations who are the representatives of the state.

There has been a move for all of millennia to destroy the nation of Israel and any remembrance of her as a nation. The most recent instance was when Adolf Hitler tried to exterminate the Jews during World War II. Because Israel is the key to end time prophecy, the warfare in heaven will only intensify as the end draws near. The Bible mentions the desire of other nations to rid themselves of Israel from the face of the earth.

For behold, Your enemies make a tumult; and those who hate You have lifted up their head. They have taken crafty counsel against Your people, and consulted together against Your sheltered ones. They have said, "Come, and *let us cut them off from being a nation,* that the name of Israel may be remembered no more." For they have consulted together with one consent; they form a confederacy against You (Psalms 83:2-5).

God clearly has enemies—particularly when it comes to the nation of Israel. As that Scripture clearly indicates, there are some who have wanted to annihilate the nation of Israel altogether. Note that those who have come against Israel have really come against God Himself. To this day that is the case. God is displeased with such action, and the Psalmist says that it is a conspiracy against God. That's because of the warfare in the heavens. What happens here on earth is a reflection of what is transpiring in the heavens. There is continual warfare between the good and the evil principalities and powers over Israel and over the nations of the world.

Even if a nation remained neutral concerning Israel, they could miss out on God's blessing and even be accused by God of standing on the sidelines and doing nothing to help Israel in their time of need. It's a biblical obligation for nations—particularly those of status and power—to help Israel. We see a similar story in Obadiah when God had an indictment against Edom, who were descendents of Esau, the brother of Jacob (Israel). God was upset with them for their bias and neutrality when their own brothers, the children of Israel, and their land were being destroyed by the Babylonians. They were deceived into thinking that they could sit by and not raise a hand to help them, and then join in to help plunder them and turn them over to their enemies.

> For violence against your brother Jacob, shame shall cover you, and you shall be cut off forever. In the day that you stood on the other side—in the day that strangers carried captive his forces, when foreigners entered his gates and cast lots for Jerusalem—even you were as one of them. But you should not have gazed on the day of your brother in the day of his captivity; nor should you have rejoiced over the children of Judah In the day of their destruction; nor should you have spoken proudly

in the day of distress. You should not have entered the gate of My people in the day of their calamity. Indeed, you should not have gazed on their affliction in the day of their calamity, nor laid hands on their substance in the day of their calamity. You should not have stood at the crossroads to cut off those among them who escaped; nor should you have delivered up those among them who remained in the day of distress (Obadiah 10-14).

The nations that oppose Israel or stand by in neutrality or help their enemies will have to face the judgment of God. God will hold those nations accountable, just as He did the nation of Edom as mentioned in the book of Obadiah. The reputation, authority, and power of such nations are always on the line when they turn their back on Israel.

The nation of Israel being restored to their land is not an accident or an aberration. They are there for the purpose of God and for the end times. How could the nation of Israel be rebirthed after nearly 1900 years of being scattered over the face of the earth, and for what reason are they back? It is God's master plan, and it is nothing short of a miracle and a victory for the godly principalities and powers. God is using this miracle as a sign for the end times—that His Son is coming soon!

The problem for the world today is that nations have abused the covenant people of the Old Testament and have taken them from their land. Time and time again, they have divided that covenant land. God will deal with that situation in the future. Even though the Bible has predicted that the children of Israel would have continual trouble throughout the years of their existence, God is very displeased with what the nations of the world have done with the people of Israel and with Canaan.

If we think for one moment that God has forgotten His promises that He made to Isaac in the book of Genesis, we need to think again. Despite their horrid disobedience in the Bible and throughout history, God will use Israel to bring about His will and His plan. Just as God has not forgotten the church despite her many failures over the past 2,000 years, God has not forgotten Israel nor has He forsaken them.

> Thus says the Lord, who gives the sun for a light by day, the ordinances of the moon and the stars for a light by night, who disturbs the sea, and its waves roar (the Lord of hosts is His name): "If those ordinances depart from before Me, says the Lord, then the seed of Israel shall also cease from being a nation before Me forever." Thus says the Lord: "If heaven above can be measured, and the foundations of the earth searched out beneath, I will also cast off all the seed of Israel for all that they have done, says the Lord" (Jeremiah 31:35-37).

While the children of Israel were in captivity in the days of Babylon, God had promised them in Ezekiel 36:24 that He would take them from out of the nations and bring them to their own land again. He said that He would give them a new heart and a new spirit. That verse would find its full completion and fit more properly in a future time of restoration, such as today's time. We read of a second marvelous time of the return of Israel when it mentions the second recovery of Israel. The first return was after the Babylonian captivity 600 years before the time of Christ, and the second time was a time in the future, which happened in the twentieth century and culminated with them becoming a nation in 1948.

> It shall come to pass in that day that the Lord shall set His hand again the *second time* to recover the remnant of His people who are left, from Assyria and Egypt, from Pathros and Cush, from Elam and Shinar, from Hamath and the islands of the sea (Isaiah 11:11).

ISRAEL OR THE CHURCH

God has had a romance with this world and with the universe, and it started with Abraham's family. It expanded to the nation of Israel through whom the Gentiles were to be saved, and it finally rested upon the church that was established by Jesus Christ. This romance that God has had with the universe is the key to its success and the key to its existence. Without God's love and romance, the world is lost.

All of this controversy as to whether the church is God's elect or Israel is God's elect is only a ploy to get our attention away from God's master plan. There has been much criticism toward the nation of Israel; and many believe that they have been replaced by the church so that the church now receives the spiritual birthright promises of God. However, Israel still remains God's people and timepiece of prophecy. We can see this throughout the Old Testament, as we see this nation on numerous occasions being brought back to life by God.

So what about the statements that say the New Testament supports the replacement of the nation of Israel by the church? Many of those who believe this point to Romans 9-11 as one of their proofs. Some say that this text shows that the church is now the elect, and that Israel is no longer central in God's master plan for the end times. They also infer that the church has replaced Israel and now receives all the promises of God that were originally intended for Israel. Even this difference and division between Israel and the church is part of the warfare that the Devil is eager to keep at a boiling point among Christians.

However, Romans 9-11 unmistakably refers to both the nation of Israel and the church as being the elect. The term "election" referred to in these chapters as the nation of Israel is an important part of the foreshadowing of the church's election. Paul was writing to the Romans who were Gentiles; he could have very easily said that the church had replaced the nation of Israel. He could have told them that all of the promises of Israel now belong to the New Testament-believing Gentile Church. But that's not what he did. Certainly there are promises made to the church, but not at the expense of God's election and call of Israel.

Paul starts each chapter of Romans 9-11 with supportive statements that indicate that Israel is still central in God's thoughts and that He has not cast them off. His is a special message of prayer and hope for that nation. This means that the promises still belong to them and God still has a plan for them. Paul even emphasizes that the Jews' ruin and guilt under the law did not change the promises that God made to them.

I tell the truth in Christ, I am not lying, my conscience also bearing me witness in the Holy Spirit, that I have great sorrow and continual grief in my heart. For I could wish that I myself were accursed from Christ for my brethren, *my countrymen according to the flesh, who are Israelites, to whom pertain the adoption, the glory, the covenants, the giving of the law, the service of God, and the promises*; of whom are the fathers and from whom, according to the flesh, Christ came, who is over all, the eternally blessed God. Amen (Romans 9:1-5).

Brethren, my heart's desire and prayer to God for Israel is that they may be saved. For I bear them witness that they have a zeal for God, but not according to knowledge. For they being ignorant of God's righteousness, and seeking to establish their own righteousness, have not submitted to the righteousness of God (Romans 10:1-3).

I say then, has God cast away His people? Certainly not! For I also am an Israelite, of the seed of Abraham, of the tribe of Benjamin. God has not cast away His people whom He foreknew (Romans 11:1-2).

I say then, have they stumbled that they should fall? Certainly not! But through their fall, to provoke them to jealousy, salvation has come to the Gentiles. Now if their fall is riches for the world, and their failure riches for the Gentiles, how much more their fullness!...For if their being cast away is the reconciling of the world, what will their acceptance be but life from the dead?... And if some of the branches were broken off, and you, being a wild olive tree, were grafted in among them, and with them became a partaker of the root and fatness of the olive tree, do not boast against the branches. But if you do boast, remember that you do not support the root, but the root supports you. You will say then, "Branches were broken off that I might be grafted in." Well said. Because of unbelief they were broken off, and you stand by faith. Do not be haughty, but fear. For if God did not spare the natural branches, He may not spare you either. ...And they also, if they do not continue in unbelief, will be grafted in, for God is able to graft them in again. For if you were cut out of the olive tree which is wild by nature, and were grafted contrary to nature into a cultivated olive tree, how much more will these, who are natural branches, be grafted into their own olive tree? (Romans 11:11-12, 15, 17-21, 23-24).

If anything, Paul reaffirms that God has continued to bless Israel. As a nation and as a people, they can still be grafted back into the representative olive tree of redemption and salvation. Paul did not despise them, but rather he acknowledges that all of the promises of the Old Testament still belonged to them. He doesn't say that the Word of God did not reach the Gentiles; but he says that according to a sovereign God, the Gentiles were saved and were now part of the church because of what happened to Israel. This happened without Israel losing any of the original covenant promises that God made to them. Not only do we have the powerful unconditional promises made to Israel in Genesis, but it is repeated by the Psalmist:

> He remembers His covenant forever, the word which He commanded, for a thousand generations, the covenant which He made with Abraham, and His oath to Isaac, and confirmed it to Jacob for a statute, to Israel as an everlasting covenant, saying, "To you I will give the land of Canaan as the allotment of your inheritance" (Psalm 105:8-11).

I believe that if Israel had obeyed God, God could have called the Gentiles through the nation of Israel. The Messiah could have come for them and from them, and there would have been no rejection of Jesus Christ by the Jews. The crucifixion could have still happened, fulfilling the Old Testament types and promises of the Messiah as our sacrifice, but perhaps implicating the Roman government only. After all, Jesus came to the Jews first and attempted to give them the message from His Father in heaven. John 1:11 says, "He came unto His own, and His own received Him not" (KJV). Unfortunately, they did reject Him. Finally, Paul went on to say about the gospel in Romans 1:16 that "It is the power of God unto salvation to everyone that believeth; to the Jew first, and also to the Greek" (KJV).

There was a place for the Jews. They had their opportunity for messianic redemption to come through them, but they missed it. I believe that if they had received Jesus, there would not have been the need for the church, as we know it today. The church could have been a part of a massive connection to the Jewish people with the nation of Israel leading the way in a great undertaking of the gospel. As it is, many Jewish people have found Christ and are part of the church without the official backing of their nation. In the future time of the millennium, the Jewish people as a nation will help rule the earth during the reign of Christ.

If only Israel had been obedient from the very start. If only they had followed Christ and believed in Him; they could have avoided all their troubles and persecution over the past 2,000 years. The promises that the church now enjoys that specifically apply to them could have been applied to Israel as well. But alas, on Paul's first missionary journey in the city of Antioch, Paul and Barnabas decided to turn to the Gentiles after their message was rejected by the Jews. Of course, this was good news to the Gentiles.

> Then Paul and Barnabas grew bold and said, "It was necessary that the word of God should be spoken to you first; but since you reject it, and judge yourselves unworthy of everlasting life, behold, we turn to the Gentiles" (Acts 13:46).

The Old Testament is filled with Scriptures that promise that God wanted to reach beyond the Jews to the Gentiles and that salvation would come to them as well, and God could have used the Jews to do that. Yet God continually reached out His hand to His covenant people, Israel. When the Messiah did come, it was because of the nation of Israel and the promise God made to them which in turn blessed the church. The covenant that God made with Abraham that many nations would be blessed through him was passed down through the Jews and to the church, and to nations around the world. The church has not replaced the nation of Israel, but what this great promise did was to give God the victory in warfare over the Devil as the church was included as part of the children of Abraham.

> Even as Abraham believed God, and it was accounted to him for righteousness. Know ye therefore that they which are of faith, the same are the children of Abraham. And the scripture, foreseeing that God would justify the heathen through faith, preached before the gospel unto Abraham, saying, In thee shall all nations be blessed. So then they which be of faith are blessed with faithful Abraham (Galatians 3:6-9 KJV).

In fact, Paul had something clear and precise to say about the gospel being a message for the Jew and Gentile—a message he said had been in the heart of God since He first instituted Israel as a nation. That is, God wanted to reach the entire world with His messianic message. When we preach the gospel message, we know that behind our message to the Gentiles in the church is a message to the Jews as well. In Ephesians 2 and 3, Paul continues to show that the message to the Gentiles is an outgrowth of the promises made to Israel. To destroy the promises made to the Jews would destroy the very foundation upon which the church has been established.

> Therefore remember that you, once Gentiles in the flesh—who are called Uncircumcision by what is called the Circumcision made in the flesh by hands—that at that time you were without Christ, being aliens from the commonwealth of Israel and strangers from the covenants of promise, having no hope and without God

in the world. But now in Christ Jesus you who once were far off have been brought near by the blood of Christ.

For He Himself is our peace, who has made both one, and has broken down the middle wall of separation, having abolished in His flesh the enmity, that is, the law of commandments contained in ordinances, so as to create in Himself one new man from the two, thus making peace, and that He might reconcile them both to God in one body through the cross, thereby putting to death the enmity. And He came and preached peace to you who were afar off and to those who were near. For through Him we both have access by one Spirit to the Father.

Now, therefore, you are no longer strangers and foreigners, but fellow citizens with the saints and members of the household of God, having been built on the foundation of the apostles and prophets, Jesus Christ Himself being the chief cornerstone, in whom the whole building, being fitted together, grows into a holy temple in the Lord, in whom you also are being built together for a dwelling place of God in the Spirit (Ephesians 2:11-22).

In Romans 11, Paul basically said that the failure of the Jews led to the opening of the door to the Gentiles. He said that their slumber and blinded eyes were for the riches of the Gentiles, and that there would be a time of fullness for Israel. He reminds the Gentiles in Rome that Israel was still the root of the tree and the Gentiles were just the branches. This does point to a plan by God to bring Israel back as part of His plan in the end times.

For I do not desire, brethren, that you should be ignorant of this mystery, lest you should be wise in your own opinion, that blindness in part has happened to Israel until the fullness of the Gentiles has come in. And so all Israel will be saved, as it is written:

"The Deliverer will come out of Zion, and He will turn away ungodliness from Jacob; for this is My covenant with them, when I take away their sins."

Concerning the gospel they are enemies for your sake, but concerning the election they are beloved for the sake of the fathers. For the gifts and the calling of God are irrevocable (Romans 11:25-29).

Indisputably, Israel remains in line to receive the unconditional covenant promises that God gave them in Genesis, just as God gave promises to the Arab world. For us to deny the promises to Israel and the possession of their land would be to deny the possession of land for the Arab world. This unconditional promise has been made to Israel, even though they have repeatedly disobeyed God and have not always walked in His ways but have walked in willful sin. They have been disobedient over the centuries of the Old Testament, and even at the time of Christ, they rejected Him and crucified Him. As far as the promises to the Arab people are concerned, they still have their land, despite the fact that they became involved with the religion of Islam, and they too have not accepted Jesus as the Messiah.

The promises from God to both these two great peoples of the sons of Isaac and the sons of Ishmael are still in effect today. God has not forgotten what He originally promised to them in the book of Genesis. God will not go back on His word.

YOU MUST GET THESE THINGS RIGHT

When it comes to the book of Genesis, there are certain things that you must get correct if you are to understand God's plan in the rest of His Word. If you don't get a good understanding about them in Genesis, you won't get it right anywhere else. It is certainly not in the spiritual understanding of His plans for His creative people or in the historical understanding of the nations and God's plan for them. These things are a part of the spiritual warfare that we are involved with continually.

Here are some examples. If you don't get a correct understanding about creation in the book of Genesis, then you will be off balance in other ways. There are Christians who can believe the entire Bible as being accurate and inspired by God. However, when it comes to the six literal days of creation and the seventh day of rest by God in Genesis 1 and 2, they have doubts about it. They have been entirely influenced by Charles Darwin's theory of evolution. Darwin's *On the Origin of Species*, published in 1859, brought about a general scientific consensus of creation through evolution and natural selection by the twentieth century. It is a theory that is opposed to the idea of all things being created by God after its own kind, a belief that has been around for thousands of years. Therefore, if you embrace evolution, you will not have a clear understanding about all of God's created beings and His ultimate plan for them and God's master plan for the world.

Even Moses believed in the seven literal days of creation when he wrote about it in the book of Exodus. These Scriptures written by Moses supporting the seven days of creation are literally the foundation for the entire covenant system of Judaism, which is based on the seventh day Sabbath. Moses used it in his teaching about resting on the seventh day just as God did after the sixth creative day. Moses said:

> For in six days the Lord made the heavens and the earth, the sea, and all that is in them, and rested the seventh day. Therefore the Lord blessed the Sabbath day and hallowed it (Exodus 20:11).

> Therefore the children of Israel shall keep the Sabbath, to observe the Sabbath throughout their generations as a perpetual covenant. It is a sign between Me and the children of Israel forever; for in six days the Lord made the heavens and the earth, and on the seventh day He rested and was refreshed (Exodus 31:16-17).

Another issue is marriage. If you don't understand its institution in the book of Genesis about marriage, then you won't understand it anywhere else in the Bible; and you certainly will not gain a correct perspective in our secular, hedonistic, and sinful world. It is important to believe that in the administrative responsibility of procreation, God established marriage between a man and a woman in order to ensure the continuance of the species. God allowed no place for homosexual behavior in His original creation.

The plan of redemption is another area we should understand first in Genesis where it began immediately following the fall of Adam and Eve into sin. In order to fully grasp God's mercy, grace, and redemption, your eyes must be opened to see that God must have had a plan to combat sin and the Devil—even before the plan was necessary. This plan of redemption involved spiritual warfare. God faced the Devil immediately and God said to him:

> And I will put enmity between you and the woman, and
> between your seed and her Seed; He shall bruise your
> head, and you shall bruise His heel (Genesis 3:15).

We have already mentioned the story of Eve, but it bears repeating at this point. She was the first to fall victim to the trickery of the Devil, but she was the first one God picked through whom the redemptive plan should come. Her offspring which produced the Messiah would be at spiritual odds with the demonic forces that were behind Satan, hence spiritual warfare. Satan's injury because of the messianic plan would be fatal; his fate is to spend eternity in the lake of fire. The injury received by Christ on the cross would be an injury that would be recoverable through His resurrection. This was God's redemptive plan through His mercy and grace. If you don't understand it fully in Genesis, if you do not see that there is no other way to God other than His plan of redemption, you might try to find other ways to God and sidestep His redemptive plan, the one found throughout the Bible.

Finally, it you don't understand God's plan for Israel through the book of Genesis, you won't have His foundation for what is written in the rest of the Bible. While it is true that Israel has not had full possession of their original given land over the years, God has not forgotten them. The covenant that God made with Isaac in the book of Genesis is still in full force just as the covenant that God made with Ishmael is still in full force. This controversy between the descendants of these two brothers will be a part of the climax in the book of Revelation called Armageddon. They, along with other nations, will be a part of the confrontation of the nations that will consume the world when Jesus Christ returns.

There is a battle being waged in the heavenly realm; and in part, it is about these four biblical injunctions. Spiritual warfare is being waged over the means of creation, marriage, redemption, and prophecy. We must fight for and protect the truth and sanctity of these God-given blessings. God wants you to be involved in fervent prayer over these issues. Now is the time to uphold these important matters in prayer, and wage war against the principalities and powers who have distorted them by opposing God. These are the things that we must pray and believe in—just as the Bible teaches them, because the lack of their Biblical emphasis is destructive to any people and nation.

With God's prophetic plan in place, we know that He has kept the national name of Israel for His chosen people. After the Lord returns to the earth, He will judge the nations of the world. Some of these nations will keep their national names and enter the millennium and participate in God's kingdom of nations for that time. Others will lose their names and will not enter the millennium, but be lost as nations forever. The name "Israel" was given by God to that nation as part of an irrevocable and unconditional promise to the sons of Abraham, Isaac, and Jacob.

Israel has been in and out as a nation because of the spiritual warfare in the heavens. They have occupied their homeland and they have lost it. According to Deuteronomy 27 and 28, they would be blessed because of their obedience and they would be cursed because of their disobedience. For that, and because they rejected Christ the Messiah when He came, they lost their homeland for nearly 1900 years until 1948. Still, they remain God's people and His timepiece of prophecy.

Similarly, for the past 2,000 years, the church has not always been obedient, but has backslidden, been lukewarm and cold, and has not always walked in the Spirit or in the ways of God. The seven churches mentioned in Revelation 2 and 3 show the various disobedient ways of the church. Today, the colossal failure in the church is shown through the outright disobedience and rebellion of its people against authority without a just reason or cause. There are people in the church who rebel against the leaders of the church without scriptural support or justification. Romans 16:17 warns us: "note those who cause divisions and offenses, contrary to the doctrine which you learned, and avoid them."

The church has fallen prey to the devices and wickedness of Satan in a spirit of pride, anger, and rebellion. Yet they remain God's people and part of His plan to be His witness in a fallen world until the Lord comes for them. The nation of Israel remains part of God's plan for the end times as well.

THE PURPOSE OF SUPERPOWERS

The term "superpower" is a relatively modern term that has been used to define nations of the twentieth century, such as England, the former USSR, and the United States. There have also been attempts to use this term retrospectively for other nations of the distant past, like Egypt; Assyria; Babylon; Persia; Greece; China; India; the Roman Empire; the Mongolian, Portuguese, and Spanish empires; and the Ottoman Empire.

While it is difficult to clearly define what constitutes a superpower, some criteria can be applied to nations that seem to fit into this category. The basis for using this term lies in their power in military, economic, political, and cultural ways that affect a great portion of the world. Superpowers generally have a global strategy with universal influence.

Some of these nations have seemed to do right things, while other nations have committed evil trespasses against God and His morality and authority. Some have been anti-god and antichrist in nature. Some have attempted to live in peace, while others have excessively expanded themselves and have aggressively dominated other nations through their superiority. They have expanded war and aggression in the world through selfishness and arrogance, and have killed and maimed millions upon millions of people throughout the history of the world. These wars on the earth however have been a mirror of the wars in the heavens between the principalities and powers.

Despite all of that, God has definitely been in control of, and concerned with, the nations of the world and particularly these superpowers since the beginning of creation. Why does it seem that certain superpowers have existed to dominate certain regions of God's planet, and what has been God's purpose in allowing them to exist? More importantly, what part do they all play in the power struggles in the atmosphere of spiritual warfare?

One reason has been clear in regard to God's relation with these superpowers. It has been revealed in the book of Genesis that an irrevocable and unconditional promise had been made to Abraham. God made a covenant plan with Abraham's family and through extension of that promise "all the families of the world would be blessed." These families became nations and some of them became superpowers who eventually had great impact upon the nation of Israel that had become chosen of God through Abraham's son, Isaac, and his grandson, Jacob.

These nations have had a responsibility toward the land of Israel because of the covenant God made with Israel in Genesis. God has a master plan for the end of the world and He is using the nation of Israel as the keystone nation to bring about this plan. Israel has been the only nation that has had an unconditional promise as part of their religious and national covenant written in the Word of God.

As stated earlier, the nations who oppose them or stand by in neutrality or help their enemies will have to face the judgment of God. This holds true for the United States as one of the latest superpowers to be involved with Israel. This is all a part of the struggle of the nations and a part of the spiritual warfare in the heavens.

In order to accomplish His plans for Israel, God uses these nations. With that purpose in mind, we know that *God always, always uses superpowers.* Generally speaking, many of the world's major superpowers have had something to do with the nation of Israel, both good and bad. Because of the Diaspora, many Jews fled to many of these distant nations. Also, some of the superpowers of the distant past invaded the land of the Jews.

As far as Israel is concerned, these powers have been there to either bless them or curse them. God has used these nations to protect them, to help them, or to discipline them. God has used them to take Israel from their land or allow them to return to their land. These events have been foisted upon that tiny nation and have happened—all because of Israel's disobedience and willful sin as a nation. The struggle over Israel that is played out on the earth mirrors the struggle between the principalities and powers in the heavens between good and evil.

The nations that have wielded such power over Israel have been:

1. Egypt, who enslaved Israel for over 400 years in the land of Egypt before Moses was called of God to deliver them;

2. Assyria, who invaded the northern land of Israel and carried ten of their twelve tribes out of their land, never to return or to be restored again;

3. Babylon, who invaded the southern land of Israel and brought the tribe of Judah into captivity into the land of Babylon for seventy years;

4. Persia, who let the Medes come in to destroy Babylon, allowed the Jews to return to their land after seventy years through an edict issued by King Cyrus;

5. Greece, who after the death of their king, Alexander the Great, brought much destruction and abomination to Jerusalem, when a descendent of one of his generals desecrated the temple by sacrificing a pig on the altar;

6. Rome, who occupied the territory of Israel and had much to do with the death of Jesus Christ;

7. The Arab peoples, who with their Islamic faith and along with the Ottoman Empire, also occupied the land of Israel until the end of World War I when the Ottoman Empire disintegrated after they lost that war;

8. England, who took over the territory of modern day Palestine at the end of World War I and allowed the Jews to begin to return to the land of Israel;

9. The United States, who inherited from England the responsibility of protecting the nation of Israel and has fought two world wars in the twentieth century in order to ensure Israel's rebirth and stability.

The problem for all of these superpowers is that they all began in great strength, but eventually came to an end. Superpowers seem to rise for an extended period of time, and then disappear from that status. Many times their failure and demise is due to:

1. Grave internal immorality that cannot be changed because the course of direction in that nation has been severely altered from its earlier convictions due to sin.

2. Horrible economic conditions that weaken the nation and which usually impact the world.

3. A warlike machine that overstretches their military and causes a lack of desire in that nation to fight in future wars.

4. Cultural differences that are good for a time, but then marginalize the various people groups in the nation and fracture its unity, authority, and power.

5. Polarization of the political powers between those who are in office and have the majority in any presiding political body, and those who are the minority and oppose the policies of the presiding majority.

Usually these five conditions along with many others are the result of a nation that has not lived for God or has turned their back on God. At one point a nation may serve God with good intentions, but soon it will lose its way and revert to sin and unrighteous living. This is because succeeding generations forget what their forefathers believed in, and they consequently contribute to the failure of the nation. This is all a result of the influences of evil principalities and powers over the nation.

Righteousness exalteth a nation: but sin is a reproach to any people (Proverbs 14:34).

With that in mind, here are some facts and observations about superpowers that lose their way and forget about God and whose superpower status changes. They are greatly impacted by spiritual warfare in heaven.

1. **No superpower in the history of the world has ever remained a superpower.** Great nations that have become superpowers have come and gone from the international scene. They fail due to the reasons mentioned in the previous paragraphs. Some have retained their national names and identities and some have not. This includes all of the following great superpowers: Egypt, Assyria, Babylon, Persia, Greece, the Roman Empire, the Ottoman Empire, England, France, Germany, and the USSR. The current superpower, the United States, is next in this great decline that will once again change the face of the world.

2. **When God is finished using a superpower, He throws them on the superpower trash heap of history.** God uses these superpowers; but when they lose their status and no longer walk with God, God will then use the next nation. The greater purpose is His master plan for the culmination of time here on this planet as He wins the victory over evil in this world. He uses the powers of the nations of this world to accomplish that purpose. God has a broader plan, and that includes the creation of a new heaven and a new earth as described in Revelation 21:1: "Now

I saw a new heaven and a new earth, for the first heaven and the first earth had passed away. Also there was no more sea."

3. **The great shifts of superpowers are focused on Israel and God's master plan for the end of the world.** God uses superpowers for a purpose and for a time, part of which is the protection of His plan for the children of Israel. As already mentioned, God gave an irrevocable and unconditional promise to Abraham in Genesis that was passed on to his son, Isaac, and his grandson, Jacob, who became the father of the nation of Israel. One reason for each time the superpower status passes from one nation to another is for the purpose of interaction with the nation of Israel, whether for good or for ill.

This holds true for the United States. The reason for its rise to superpower status was to be a part of that long list of nations that have had some impact and influence on the nation of Israel. The United States revolted against another superpower, England, to gain their independence. Within approximately 175 years, England was going to come to an end as a superpower. Therefore, God needed another great nation to replace them for the end times—all for the purpose of bringing Israel back to her homeland.

The United States gained their independence in 1776 through a declaration followed by a number of years of war with England. Then they fought a Civil War to become a great nation by defeating the issue of slavery and remaining a unified nation that was to be "under God." They were able to become a superpower and join with their allies to fight two world wars to ensure the return of the nation of Israel to her rightful place in the Middle East.

How has God dealt with these nations—including the United States—today? Why do they rise in power and then seem to fall from God's grace? The answer is found in God's Word. To repeat a story given in a previous chapter, the prophet Jeremiah was asked to go the potter's house and observe the work of the potter on the wheel. The work of pottery was remade on the potter's wheel. This was an analogy of the nation of Israel and the nations of the world. It shows what God will do if a nation turns from evil or if a nation turns to evil. It also shows God's planned impending disaster if they do evil. Again, the prophet writes:

> Then the word of the Lord came to me, saying: "O house of Israel, can I not do with you as this potter?" says the Lord. "Look, as the clay is in the potter's hand, so are you in My hand, O house of Israel! The instant I speak concerning a nation and concerning a kingdom, to pluck up, to pull down, and to destroy it, if that nation against whom I have spoken turns from its evil, I will relent of the disaster that I thought to bring upon it. And the instant I speak concerning a nation and concerning a kingdom, to build and to plant it, if it does evil in My sight so that it does not obey My voice, then I will relent concerning the good with which I said I would benefit it. Now therefore, speak to the men of Judah and to the inhabitants of Jerusalem, saying, "Thus says the Lord: 'Behold, I am fashioning a disaster and devising a plan against you. Return now everyone from his evil way, and make your ways and your doings good.'" And they said, "That is hopeless! So we will walk according to our own plans, and we will every one obey the dictates of his evil heart" (Jeremiah 18:5-12).

With that Scripture from Jeremiah 18 in mind, we can see that God will bring judgment on America just as He has done with any other nation that has turned its back on God as we have. A lot can be said about the leadership of our presidents, Congress, and the court system, and how they have led us down the wrong course and far from God. Over the course of the 236 plus years of the existence of the United States, both good and bad can be said about all of our leadership. One thing we do know, the Bible says that God allows leadership in any country to rise and fall at His biding.

With our nation in serious financial, military, and moral trouble since the middle of the twentieth century, our presidents have been appointed by God to preside over a nation that is collapsing right before our eyes. Other presidents in the future will have to deal with the same consequences as America has turned its back on a faithful and loving God. This is the time to fervently pray for our country and our leaders. This is the time to ask God to send a mighty revival and a spiritual outpouring of His Spirit, His grace, and His mercy. All people of faith can pray that our country will turn back to Him.

THE CONSEQUENCES OF WAR

War is hellish! It is one of the most brutal acts of humankind. War has been responsible not only for millions of soldiers killed and wounded, but countless numbers of innocent civilians who are caught in the middle of the conflagration. War kills, maims, and brings disaster on nations, yet it is something that God uses to accomplish His will because of man's disobedience and sin.

Man has not followed God, and because of that, has been embroiled in war. It is one of the signs of the end times mentioned in Matthew 24. War on earth is definitely a reflection of the warfare in the heavens as the principalities and powers struggle over the territory on the earth and how much influence they can have over each individual nation. Evil angels try to impose their territorial rights while the godly angels want to hold on to the territory that belongs to God. The godly angels want peace on earth among the nations and the evil angels want war and insurrection. That's why it is imperative that any nation prays, follows God, and remains true to their calling.

God said to King Asa, the third king of Judah, that he would have wars for foolishly not relying on God. Asa made a good effort in the early years of his reign to listen to the voice of God through the prophets by removing the idols that were in the land and by entering into a covenant with the Lord. Yet in the latter years of his rule, he sought the help of the king of Syria against his brothers who were in the northern kingdom of

Israel. God was very displeased, and King Asa was told by the prophet Hanani that he had not relied on the Lord. The prophet said that God watches over those who are loyal to Him. Asa was told that he was foolish for not consulting God:

> For the eyes of the Lord run to and fro throughout the whole earth, to show Himself strong on behalf of those whose heart is loyal to Him. In this you have done foolishly; *therefore from now on you shall have wars* (2 Chronicles 16:9).

King Asa was rebuked because He did not trust in God. King Asa foolishly relied on man to help him with his battles against his enemies. The northern kingdom of Israel who were Judah's brothers were not serving God but were serving idols, and King Asa should have relied on God and God would have helped him defeat the evil king of Israel. As a result of his foolishness, the king was going to have continual war.

This principle is still at work today. Since the times of the Bible, there have been numerous wars—some have accomplished much, but some have accomplished little. Throughout history, nations have used conflicts to solve differences. Throughout history, there has been increasing sophistication in combat, but war's ability to change the world has had little success. The world has remained the same in terms of peace.

Some wars are of little significance while others are world-changing. There have been many wars, including the Persian wars, the Roman wars, the Crusades, the Hundred Years War, the War of the Roses, the Thirty Years War, the Seven Years War, the French Revolution, the Napoleonic Wars, the Crimean War, and the Franco-Prussian War, just to mention a few. These wars have basically involved aggression due to rival claims to power, control over lands, and the seizing of lands by other nations. Wars are a result of man's insatiable desire to fight, dominate, hate, and murder. Man has brought destruction and mayhem to every part of the world where he has lived.

Intergalactic Warfare

God has therefore allowed a culture of war to exist and has used it throughout history, using man's evil ways to move the nations of the world into proper alignment before the end of time. War was also there to deal with man's sin. Many warmongering men of the past were bullies who wanted attention, but were only insignificantly biting at the heels of history as footnotes in a distant past. God allowed them to be used by Satan to foment disobedience, disorder, and chaos in the world as a means of punishment. Nations and religions were revolutionized as attention was shifted to the powers of the Western world in order to prolong God's timing and prepare the world for the end times.

Something can be seen in some of the conflicts since the fall of Jerusalem in AD 70. Besides all the wars for control of people and land, there have been wars that have had a direct impact on the nation of Israel. After AD 70, Israel lost its land because of their direct involvement in the crucifixion of Jesus, the Son of God, who was sent to them. Israel did not trust in God nor did they believe that God had sent the Messiah. Because of their disbelief, their land was eventually taken over by the Arab world, who as sons of Ishmael, were now involved with the Islamic faith. They invaded the land of Israel and captured parts of the old Christian Holy Roman Empire.

Within the Holy Roman Empire itself, alliances had been made between the pope and the emperors. The pope and the empire remained closely associated for hundreds of years. The popes sought protection from the emperors and the emperors sought the blessing of being crowned in order to have recognition among the masses of people. These were unholy alliances by people of faith with unrighteous leaders of the nations of Europe. It deepened the crisis of spiritual warfare in the heavens over Europe as the Holy Roman Empire was revived. The Devil was ready to strike another bloody blow to the beleaguered and scattered covenant people of God. An ominous shadow of war, persecution, and hatred was ready to be cast over Europe because the religious people of God made an unholy alliance with the demonic forces in the heavens through the emperors with whom they conspired.

These alliances eventually led to the Germanic division of the Roman Empire. It brought about the First Reich (a Germanic term for empire or kingdom) under King Otto in AD 962 and the Second Reich in 1871 through the influence of Otto Von Bismarck. Bismarck died in 1898, but this kingdom continued until the end of the First World War in 1918. During the Third Reich under Adolf Hitler, the spiritual warfare that the Devil had with God and His people in Europe brought about the horrible persecution and murder of six million of God's Jewish chosen people.

Part of this warfare over Europe brought about the Crusades which were a series of attempts by the church from approximately AD 1095-1270 to win back the land of Palestine and other biblical sites for the Christian world. The Crusades were military marches encouraged by European Christians on behalf of the papacy in Rome. They were attempts to regain control of the lands that the Muslim had taken from the Christian world through military conquest hundreds of years earlier. Overall, the Crusades were incited by the spiritual warfare in the heavens and by the fleshly desire for war on earth. They were basically considered unsuccessful.

The reason they were unsuccessful was that it was not God's time to win the land of Israel back for His master plan. It was attempted through the efforts of, and for the power of, the emperor and the church, and not for the glory of God and His promise to Israel. God needed more time to work out a time of continual dealing with Israel and the nations of the world. Israel needed to be brought back through other means and other efforts. The means He intended were wars far in the future in the twentieth century. The wars of our last century set the stage for God to bring about the changes necessary for the end times.

God planned a time for the Jews to return to their land. World War I gave the Jews such an opportunity. At the time of World War I, the Islamic people of the Ottoman Empire had occupied the land of Israel since the sixteenth century. When World War I began, the already weakened Ottoman Empire sided with the Central Powers of Germany and Austria-Hungary. They fought against the Allied Powers of France, Britain, the United States, Russia, Japan, Italy, and other nations. The

Allied Powers won and the Central Powers lost the war; as a result, the Ottoman Empire disintegrated and lost the land of Palestine. This was accomplished by the will of God in order to prepare the world for the events of the end times.

This opened the door for the Jews to return to the land of Palestine, especially after the British Balfour Declaration of 1917. Then Foreign Secretary Arthur James Balfour issued a formal statement on behalf of the British government indicating Britain's support for a national homeland for the Jews in Palestine. This led to the 1922 League of Nations mandate that the land of Palestine be given to Britain. This encouraged the Jews to return to Palestine, and they did so over the years that followed.

World War II followed, which was I believe was an extension of World War I. Dissatisfaction among the German people about the reparations required of them after the First World War gave rise to the leader, Adolf Hitler. During World War II, Hitler killed millions of Jews and his action required God to step in to save His people before the end times. With God using both good and evil as the Bible indicates, he used both the godly nations of America and Britain as well as the anti-Christian nation of the USSR to crush Hitler. After Hitler was defeated, the United Nations, which was more pro-western at the time, was sympathetic toward the Jewish people; and in 1947, they allowed the land of Palestine to be partitioned between the Arabs who had been living there, and the Jewish people who were arriving every year. Then in 1948, the Jews declared statehood and Israel became a nation once again.

There was a horrific killing of the Jews during the days of Hitler. He thought that he was doing a service for God by annihilating the Jews. There had been terrible Anti-Semitism for hundreds of years throughout Europe for many reasons, but one was because of the Jewish association with the death of Christ. Hitler thought he was doing the world a favor by ridding the world of a people he thought were useless and the source of all the world's problems. Jesus told His followers to watch out for this kind of action. Jesus said:

Yes, the time is coming that whoever kills you will think that he offers God service. And these things they will do to you because they have not known the Father nor Me (John 16:2-3).

Hitler was a maniac, but his actions happened right in the midst of the return of the Jews before the end times, and it was World War I and World War II that helped it to happen. Their return was after nearly 1900 years away from their land, without Jerusalem, and without their temple and religious sacrifices. The Jews are now back in their land in order to prepare for the future time of the great tribulation, the wrath of God, and the return of Jesus Christ at the end of the tribulation.

Other wars involving the United States and their involvement as a superpower to help prepare the world for the end times include the Korean Conflict; the Vietnam War; and the Gulf, Iraq, and Afghanistan Wars. These wars are not mistakes, nor have they gone unnoticed in God's master plan. His will is being done for the end times; and it involves massive shifts of global superpower strategy through war.

In fact, these wars are a microcosm of the great conflict between God and His archrival, Satan. They are a reflection of the massive eternal struggle that has existed between good and evil since the beginning, with the nation of Israel at the center. These conflicts have had something to do with preparing the world for the end times.

1. The Korean Conflict has obstructed the powers of the East until the day they will eventually march into Israel as mentioned in Revelation 16:12. If these powers, which include China and North Korea, had continued unchecked, who could guess how far they would have continued in their quest for domination? Decades after this conflict, only a truce has been established at the 38th parallel between North and South Korea. The empires of China and Korea have been around for thousands of years, and could someday rise with other nations from the East, such as Afghanistan and Pakistan that we have been involved in with war. They could all rise in great power to fulfill the Scripture

mentioned in Revelation as the land of the Middle East will once again be at the center of attention. As for now, they remain stopped within the will of God until the final days of the invasion of Israel. These nations remain in check thanks to the Korean Conflict and the involvement of America in that part of the world.

2. The Vietnam War helped finalize the collapse of the USSR and helped fulfill what will eventually happen according to Ezekiel 38 and 39. In the last days, armies from the north, which includes parts of the old USSR, will invade the land of Israel during the tribulation. The Soviet Union, who for decades had pumped millions of dollars into their war machine, ignored the financial needs and the economic struggle of the people they had dominated for decades. Politically and economically, the USSR collapsed and their vast empire came to an end. Their involvement in the Vietnam War helped to finalize that. They collapsed as a superpower fifteen years after the end of the Vietnam War. Had they remained a superpower, they probably would have marched into Israel all alone and not have been able to fulfill those chapters. Now that they are no longer a superpower, they have made alliances and friendships with nations in Europe. This brings them in line with Ezekiel 38 and 39 which says that a number of nations from the North, the South, and from Eastern Europe will invade Israel in the last days. These nations will include people from nations such as Germany, Iran, Ethiopia, Libya, and Egypt. They are all now in a position to fulfill this prophecy within God's prophetic timetable, thanks to the Vietnam War and the resolve of America, even though many protested the war at that time.

3. The Gulf and Iraq Wars and our involvement in Afghanistan in the 1990s and early 2000 have helped weaken the vast superpower status of the United States, and send it into economic turmoil. As the last remaining superpower coming out of the Second World War, we are on the verge of collapse just like the other great

superpowers of the past. Will there always be an America? I'm sure, yes, but the economic collapse of the United States will help bring a superpower shift back to the Middle East, Europe, and the Far East in preparation for the end times. God is bringing the world one step closer to major times of difficulty and fulfillment as mentioned in the Bible.

All of this helps us to understand the struggle of principalities and powers over the nations and what will happen as God finishes the prophetic clock for all time. We now know that all of the nations of the world, like never before in history, are all in place for the coming of the Lord. Nations will come from the East, North, South, and West for the battle of Armageddon. God has readied the world for His Son to return to the earth and lay claim to His creation. The world is like a ticking time bomb, and it is Jesus who will return and fight in a glorious battle over the nations.

We now know the answers to these questions: "Who has control over the nations of the world and when does their time of power begin and when does it end?"; "Who controls their boundaries?"; "Who controls how much territory they occupy?"; and "With all the wars of the past that we know about, will war play a part in the end when the Lord comes?"

The answer is simple and is made clear in God's Word. Four things, we know for sure.

1. God is the one who says when a nation begins and when it ends.

2. He is the one who sets its boundaries.

3. He is the one who is in charge of its leaders.

4. He is the one who will make war with the nations of the world in the end of time.

The following verses speak about how much God has control of this world.

> And [God] hath made of one blood all nations of men for to dwell on all the face of the earth, and hath determined

the times before appointed, and the bounds of their habitation (Acts 17:26).

And he changeth the times and the seasons: he removeth kings, and setteth up kings: he giveth wisdom unto the wise, and knowledge to them that know understanding (Daniel 2:21).

And I saw heaven opened, and behold a white horse; and he that sat upon him was called Faithful and True, and in righteousness he doth judge and make war (Revelation 19:11).

Chapter Six: God and the Future

INTERVENTION BY GOD

Each continent and every nation has had their moment when God has tried to reach out to them and speak to them. Many nations have had revivals in which God has moved to save them, or bring them close to Him, only to slide back into disobedience, failure, and ruin in the years to follow.

In order for our nation to turn back to God, it is not only imperative for the church to repent, it is necessary for the politicians to repent on behalf of our nation as well. In order for our nation to survive, it will require not only the spiritual leaders of the church to publicly call on God in repentance, it will require our political leaders to call for repentance as well.

Every nation needs an intervention by God. This can come about only as a nation seeks God and turns from their evil ways. A revival of spiritual fervor and of living righteously before God can only come as a people intercedes on behalf of the nation. God will step in to save the nation as it follows Him.

We need to take responsibility for our nation and pray for it. The reason we pray for our nation is because the people of the nation are greatly impacted by those who are ruling over them. In the Bible, not only was it the spiritual leaders who were held accountable to God for the life of the nation, it was the political leaders as well. No nation can return to God if the laws of the land do not reflect the biblical teachings found in God's Word. That is why the church, the spiritual arm of the nation, needs to pray for the political leaders. The Bible tells us clearly:

> I exhort therefore, that, first of all, supplications, prayers, intercessions, and giving of thanks, be made for all men; for Kings, and for all that are in authority (1 Timothy 2:1-2 KJV).

Through prayer and intercession, the church can be an overruling power in the spiritual realm of principalities and powers. This is our involvement in spiritual warfare. If the church does not pray, the responsibility for the failure in any nation will be a burden for the church. This is clear when it comes to the church and its behavior. The church must be obedient according to the will of God. The Bible says:

> But let none of you suffer as a murderer, a thief, an evildoer, or as a busybody in other people's matters. Yet if anyone suffers as a Christian, let him not be ashamed, but let him glorify God in this matter. For the time has come for judgment to begin at the house of God; and if it begins with us first, what will be the end of those who do not obey the gospel of God? Now "If the righteous one is scarcely saved, where will the ungodly and the sinner appear?" (1 Peter 4: 15-18).

As you can see from that Scripture, the church is the first to fall under the judgment of God when it comes to disobedience to God's commands. However, in the Bible it was clear that judgment also fell on those who led the nation politically. This can be seen in several instances in the Bible that involved spiritual warfare and authority of the nations.

1. God punished the nation of Israel numerous times because the kings led the nation to worship idols.

2. King David was personally punished because he committed adultery with a married woman, and then had her husband killed in battle.

3. The city of Nineveh was ready to be judged, but its king was able to save his city and nation during the time of the preaching of Jonah. He repented in sackcloth and ashes and led his people to do the same; he also rescued his nation for the next 150 years from a destruction that was coming from the hand of God.

We discover from Scripture that God is very interested in the politics of a nation. We sometimes forget that God is the one who controls its leaders. He is the one who sends messengers to them. This was the case over and over again in the Old Testament. One great example was when God sent the prophet Daniel to speak to King Nebuchadnezzar. Daniel interpreted a dream that the king had about a great image that was symbolic of the nations of the world. This is what Daniel declared:

> Daniel answered and said: "Blessed be the name of God forever and ever, for wisdom and might are His. And He changes the times and the seasons; *He removes kings and raises up kings*; He gives wisdom to the wise and knowledge to those who have understanding. He reveals deep and secret things; He knows what is in the darkness, and light dwells with Him" (Daniel 2:20-22).

Leadership of a nation is very important to God. He wishes that nations and their leaders would follow Him in obedience. Here is a similar Scripture about God's authority that can be applied to leadership:

> For exaltation comes neither from the east nor from the west nor from the south. But God is the Judge: He puts down one, and exalts another. For in the hand of the Lord there is a cup, and the wine is red; it is fully mixed, and He pours it out; surely its dregs shall all the wicked of the earth drain and drink down (Psalms 75:6-8).

America needs an outpouring of the Holy Spirit to change the lives of individuals and our nation. Until we become desperate for God to move in our nation and until we help change its course of direction, we will be a nation that will continue to move away from Him. If a people in any nation acts in a wicked manner, nothing good will be able to happen. This is where we enter into the realm of spiritual warfare and do battle with the forces of demonic spirits that are at enmity with God and who try to control the nation.

> Let God arise, let His enemies be scattered; let those also who hate Him flee before Him. As smoke is driven away, so drive them away; as wax melts before the fire, so let the wicked perish at the presence of God (Psalms 68:1-2).

WHAT ABOUT THE FUTURE?

As we have discovered, God has a plan for the future and a plan for the nation of Israel. We realize that the great shifts of superpowers are centered on Israel and God's master plan for the end of the world. We also know that God has a way of dealing with the nations. In the Old Testament, He had issues with Egypt, Assyria, and Babylon, just to mention a few.

How God brings judgment upon the nations is clearly seen in the Bible. In the book of Amos, God had serious problems with His own chosen people, the nation of Israel. He sent them numerous judgments to see if they would come back to Him, but they rebuffed His offers. They were so intent on living how they wanted to live that they forgot the God who had done so much for them in the past. They refused to repent of their sins and return to the God who loved them dearly.

> "I gave you cleanness of teeth in all your cities, and lack of bread in all your places; *yet you have not returned to Me,*" says the Lord. "I also withheld rain from you, when there were still three months to the harvest. I made it rain on one city; I withheld rain from another city. One part was rained upon, and where it did not rain the part withered. So two or three cities wandered to another city to drink water, but they were not satisfied; *yet you have not returned to Me,*" says the Lord. "I blasted you with

blight and mildew. When your gardens increased, your vineyards, your fig trees, and your olive trees, the locust devoured them; *yet you have not returned to Me,*" says the Lord. "I sent among you a plague after the manner of Egypt; your young men I killed with a sword, along with your captive horses; I made the stench of your camps come up into your nostrils; *yet you have not returned to Me,*" says the Lord. "I overthrew some of you, as God overthrew Sodom and Gomorrah, and you were like a firebrand plucked from the burning; *yet you have not returned to Me,*" says the Lord (Amos 4:6-11).

We realize that God is the one who allowed all of these catastrophes to occur because He wanted to speak to the nation through these disasters. He allows calamities to bring us to the point where we acknowledge that we are not in control, but He is. The best thing we could do would be for us to read and understand the Word of God and simply obey Him. When we do not listen to the voice of God, He will do practically anything to get our attention. He wants all of our human activities to stop, so that we realize that we are not in control. He wants us to come to the conclusion that there is a higher power and authority, and that we must give allegiance to Him as that higher power and authority. The Bible says that He is also in charge of the rain and the snow that stops man's hand. He does this because He wants us to stop our activity and acknowledge Him.

God thunders marvelously with His voice; He does great things which we cannot comprehend. For He says to the snow, "Fall on the earth"; likewise to the gentle rain and the heavy rain of His strength. *He seals the hand of every man, that all men may know His work.* The beasts go into dens, and remain in their lairs. From the chamber of the south comes the whirlwind, and cold from the scattering winds of the north. By the breath of God ice is given, and the broad waters are frozen. Also with moisture He saturates the thick clouds; He scatters His bright clouds.

And they swirl about, being turned by His guidance, that they may do whatever He commands them on the face of the whole earth. He causes it to come, whether for correction, or for His land, or for mercy (Job 37:5-13).

OH LORD, SEND A REVIVAL

If America needs anything, it is a revival. This is what we need to pray for. If we want our nation to turn around from the brink of disaster, we need to seek the face of God and ask Him to help us to return to our spiritual roots where we put God first in everything. We need to come to the point where "political correctness" isn't put above "God correctness." We need to return to what the Bible says is the correct thing to do in the nation. We long for a stirring like those that occurred as in the early days of our nation.

I understand the extreme things that can happen when a strong emphasis is placed on spirituality without tolerance to others who believe differently. Things have occurred in our spiritual nation that we are not proud of today, like the Salem witch trials, or the practice of slavery, in which some in our nation thought it was their God-given right to own slaves. These are terrible marks against the righteousness of our nation, and we categorically abhor them.

Nevertheless, we pray for revival. We pray that our nation will return to walking in holiness before the Lord. We pray that we will give God His rightful place in the choices of our nation. We pray for a stirring of every heart in America that they would turn to God for peace and joy.

There have been numerous revivals throughout the history of the world. Besides the great revivals over the centuries that included Russia and all of Asia, there were great revivals that affected the western lands of Britain, Ireland, Australia, Scandinavia, Wales, and all of Europe during the seventeenth and eighteenth centuries. All of these revivals made a major impact on the nations, and on both the Catholic and Protestant churches. People were praying, and there was a resurgence of the Spirit of God for that time.

David Siriano

The revivals of the seventeenth century as recorded in Europe eventually came to the colonies of Pennsylvania and Virginia in America in the eighteenth century. These revivals in Europe led to the First Great Awakening in America which swept the American Colonies in the 1730s and the 1740s and included the preaching of men like Jonathan Edwards and George Whitefield. There are some who believe that this revival played a key role in helping to influence the American Revolution and prepare the colonies for the Revolutionary War. The preaching of Edwards, Whitefield, and others was contrary to the common social messages of the day. They preached that the Bible taught that all men were created equal and that all men and women could be saved, regardless of their class or social status, thus helping to plant and water the seeds that birthed the revolutionary concepts of that day.

The Second Great Awakening of the nineteenth century helped America endure the Civil War and brought about the preaching of individuals including Charles Finney of the Presbyterian Church. Without the help of God and this great revival, America may never have become a superpower, and thus play a leading role in the protection of Israel into the twentieth and twenty-first centuries. Looming over America was a gigantic struggle in spiritual warfare for the survival of the nation and a revival was needed to keep America on the right spiritual track. God needed a new superpower to help guide Israel to her destiny in 1948.

A great prayer revival made an impact on the Civil War as well. It involved the soldiers on both sides, and it helped to create a positive spiritual awakening in both armies. England, who had been a superpower for centuries, was about to lose that status in the twentieth century. God looked a century into the future, and He needed America to rise to her great spiritual and political presence in the world, so it could eventually help lead and protect Israel in their land.

Demonic forces were in place to fight over the landmass of this great fledgling nation during the Civil War. Without the northern victory over slavery and its proper dismissal as an evil system, America would have been reduced to two struggling nations with no Christian influence in the world. It never would have become a great superpower to help protect Israel in the future. The issue of slavery was part of the great spiritual warfare of the heavens. The Devil wanted to continue to repress the black peoples of America, and God wanted them to be set free, hence the spiritual struggle. The North won and America continued its revolution into industry and technology to become the great power that it is today. Without that victory, America would have been a passing power of little importance.

God was ready for the twentieth century and was about to teach this new superpower some important lessons. He needed to send a message to this up-and-coming powerful nation about what He was about to do. Two great symbols of the future of America were about to unfold in 1906. These two events preceded the two great wars that loomed in its future.

First of all, on April 14th of 1906, America saw another spiritual awakening similar to the First and Second Great Awakenings of the eighteenth and nineteenth centuries. America needed another great revival to prepare her for the two great world wars that lay ahead: World War I and World War II. Many people outside of the mainstream church were part of that revival and God spared America once again because of their spiritual rebirth at that time and the prayers of God's people. This revival was the powerful Holy Spirit Revival of Azusa Street in Los Angeles, California that had a huge impact on the church throughout the twentieth century. That revival set the stage for other great revivals of the century, including the Charismatic Renewal and the Jesus People Revival, which both rocked the church, bringing a spiritual emphasis that has changed the modern day church. Those revivals awakened the church to her roots in how she worships and praises God in Spirit-filled freedom.

Just four days later on April 18, 1906, the second great symbolic event impacted America as a powerful earthquake shook San Francisco and brought a consciousness of how delicate our planet is. With the 1906 Azusa Street revival in Los Angeles and the 1906 earthquake in San Francisco just days apart, God had begun to shake our nation in a spiritual, and in a seismographic, way. The earthquake was a stinging reminder in the new century that God was still in control of the heavens and the earth. The Bible talks about how God would shake the heavens and the earth in the last days. It mentions this shaking of the earth in Haggai 2 and Isaiah 13 and 24. Similar verses in Hebrews say it all:

> See that you do not refuse Him who speaks. For if they did not escape who refused Him who spoke on earth, much more shall we not escape if we turn away from Him who speaks from heaven, whose voice then shook the earth; but now He has promised, saying, *"Yet once more I shake not only the earth, but also heaven."* Now this, *"Yet once more,"* indicates the removal of those things that are being shaken, as of things that are made, that the things which cannot be shaken may remain. Therefore, since we are receiving a kingdom which cannot be shaken, let us have grace, by which we may serve God acceptably with reverence and godly fear. For our God is a consuming fire (Hebrews 12:25-29).

The conclusion of our understanding of the great revivals in America is that God used them before great calamities took place. God used the First Great Awakening in the eighteenth century to prepare America for the Revolutionary War. He used the Second Great Awakening in the nineteenth century to prepare America for the Civil War. He used the Azusa Street Revival in the twentieth century to prepare America for World War I and World War II.

The question I have is, "What great revival does God have prepared for America in the twenty-first century to prepare her for any future calamities that may lie ahead?" Remember, God has used superpowers to influence Israel for good or evil, which is a reflection of the spiritual warfare in the heavens, and to work out His eternal master plan for the world. Therefore, He sends both revivals and calamites to whatever superpower is in place to create the influence needed to line up with His goals and His will. He will proceed with blessings and cursing upon any nation, just as He did with the nation of Israel during the days of the Bible.

Does God have a revival planned for the twenty-first century in America in preparation for some calamitous time that lies ahead? If so, is the calamitous time perhaps war, earthquakes, pestilence, or other great disasters that we may least expect? Is the second coming of Christ so close that any calamitous event in the twenty-first century would bring in the time of the end? Are we that close to the "catching away" of the church and the great tribulation that involves the Antichrist? With those questions in mind, the Church's goal should be to *proclaim a revival of an awareness of the second coming of Jesus Christ in the twenty-first century.*

CHAOS AND THE RETURN OF JESUS CHRIST

Just since the beginning of the twenty-first century, America and the world have had their share of horrific catastrophic events that have torn at the very fabric of the geologic and economic strength of society. God has warned the world in a powerful way with strong signs of instability and failure that would shake any people and any nation. Tremendous warnings have been given by God and already since the year 2000, we have seen:

1. An earthquake hit India and kills 30,000 people.

2. A terrorist attack in America in 2001 kills nearly 3,000 people.

3. An earthquake and tsunami hits Indonesia and the countries around the Indian Ocean in 2006, killing 295,000 people.

4. Hurricane Katrina lashes out at the Gulf Coast in America and kills 1,836 people.

5. An earthquake hits China and kills 50,000 people.

6. A cyclone hits Myanmar (Burma) and kills 22,000 people.

7. Economic failure strikes America and the world, the worst since the Great Depression of 1929.

8. An earthquake in Haiti leaves over 200,000 dead.

9. An earthquake, tsunami, and nuclear disaster hits Japan and kills over 15,000 people.

That list is but a fraction of the numerous disasters that have continually struck the earth since the turn of the century. We constantly see tornados, hurricanes, floods, and wars that ravage our planet day after day. God is sending message after message to this world to prepare for the end times and the second coming of His Son, Jesus Christ.

Not everyone believes in the second coming of Jesus Christ. Not everyone is living as if He is coming soon. For years people have had to give their lives as martyrs because they stood as a witness for Christ and believed in His soon return. For numerous decades now, we rarely hear messages about the coming of the Lord. Too many people have laughed at the idea.

> Knowing this first: that scoffers will come in the last days, walking according to their own lusts, and saying, "Where is the promise of His coming? For since the fathers fell asleep, all things continue as they were from the beginning of creation" (2 Peter 3:3-4).

The first coming of Christ came with many predicted signs that were given through the Old Testament prophets. When Christ was born and dedicated in the temple forty days after His birth in obedience to the law, Simeon mentioned a sign that was being revealed now that Christ was born. It is recorded that Simeon said:

> Behold, this Child is destined for the fall and rising of many in Israel, and for a *sign* which will be spoken against (yes, a sword will pierce through your own soul also), that the thoughts of many hearts may be revealed (Luke 2:34-35)

Simeon mentioned this sign as a time of difficulty and opposition for Mary and for the nation of Israel. Just as that sign was given at His first coming, the Bible says that a sign will be given at His second coming. Referring to Matthew 24 again, it mentions that a sign would be given when Christ returns to the earth. In the Greek, the word for "sign" for the second coming of Christ in Matthew 24 is the same word in the Greek used for His first coming in Luke 2:34-35. Matthew 24 states that after the great tribulation unfolds, this sign would be given when Christ literally returns to the earth.

> Then the *sign* of the Son of Man will appear in heaven, and then all the tribes of the earth will mourn, and they will see the Son of Man coming on the clouds of heaven with power and great glory (Matthew 24:30).

The Greek word found in both of those verses is *semeion*. The word means "a sign, mark, token." Also, it means "that by which a person or a thing is distinguished from others and is known."[9] We do know that when Christ appears at the second coming, all people will know that He has come. His sign will be given as He comes with power and great glory.

When considering this next big event, Christ's return, that will take place for the church, there are certain aspects that we must consider in order to be prepared for it. First of all, if we understand that the church is to be removed beforehand, why bother even studying about these awful events that will strike the earth with terrible tenacity? If the church is going to be gone, why even think about what will happen? Why put ourselves through such misery?

With that in mind, here are some reasons why we should study and prepare for the end times:

1. We are to give testimony about Jesus which is the heart and soul of prophecy until then.

> For the testimony of Jesus is the spirit of prophecy (Revelation 19:10).

2. We are to listen to what the Holy Spirit says to the church about prophecy.

> He who has an ear, let him hear what the Spirit says to the churches (Revelation 2:7, 11, 17, 29; 3:6, 13, 22).

---

9. Thayer and Smith, Greek Lexicon entry for Semeion, The KJV New Testament Greek Lexicon, accessed August 9, 2013, http://www.biblestudytools.com/lexicons/greek/kjv/semeion.html.

3. There is a blessing to those who read, hear, and keep the words of prophecy.

    Blessed is he who reads and those who hear the words of this prophecy, and keep those things which are written in it; for the time is near (Revelation 1:3).

4. So we will be comforted and not be afraid about the timing of end time events:

    Not to be soon shaken in mind or troubled, either by spirit or by word or by letter, as if from us, as though the day of Christ had come. Let no one deceive you by any means; for that Day will not come unless the falling away comes first, and the man of sin is revealed, the son of perdition (2 Thessalonians 2:2-3).

5. So that we will know the signs that the Return of Christ is soon to occur:

    And He will send His angels with a great sound of a trumpet, and they will gather together His elect from the four winds, from one end of heaven to the other. "Now learn this parable from the fig tree: When its branch has already become tender and puts forth leaves, you know that summer is near. So you also, when you see all these things, know that it is near—at the doors! Assuredly, I say to you, this generation will by no means pass away till all these things take place" (Matthew 24:31-34).

6. So that we can warn others about judgment. Enoch prophesied:

    Behold, the Lord comes 'with ten thousands of His saints, to execute judgment on all, to convict all who are ungodly among them of all their ungodly deeds which they have committed in an ungodly way, and of all the harsh things which ungodly sinners have spoken against Him (Jude 14-15).

7. It is a message that has continually blessed and strengthened the church for generations.

   The mystery which has been hidden from ages and from generations, but now has been revealed to His saints. To them God willed to make known what are the riches of the glory of this mystery among the Gentiles: which is Christ in you, the hope of glory (Colossians 1:26-27).

8. It is a relevant message that warns us about compromise with the world.

   Now the works of the flesh are evident, which are: adultery, fornication, uncleanness, lewdness, idolatry, sorcery, hatred, contentions, jealousies, outbursts of wrath, selfish ambitions, dissensions, heresies, envy, murders, drunkenness, revelries, and the like; of which I tell you beforehand, just as I also told you in time past, that those who practice such things will not inherit the kingdom of God (Galatians 5:19-21).

9. It reveals the end of history and the defeat of God's enemies.

   "Behold, I am coming as a thief. Blessed is he who watches, and keeps his garments, lest he walk naked and they see his shame." And they gathered them together to the place called in Hebrew, Armageddon (Revelation 16:15-16).

10. It shows us a picture of heaven and of the glorified Christ as part of it.

    In My Father's house are many mansions; if it were not so, I would have told you. I go to prepare a place for you. And if I go and prepare a place for you, I will come again and receive you to Myself; that where I am, there you may be also (John 14:2-3).

Matthew 24 gives us the best information about the return of Christ in the entire Bible. In this chapter after the disciples showed Christ the beauty and grandeur of the temple of Jerusalem that was built by Solomon and refurbished by Herod, Jesus said that the temple was going to be destroyed. His statement was fulfilled; the temple was destroyed in AD 70.

During this encounter with His disciples, Jesus outlined significant things that were going to happen to the nation of Israel and to the world. Jesus' statements were predicted and have made an impact upon the entire world since that time. This chapter shows us the encounter that we have in the realm of spiritual warfare from the times of Jesus until now. This warfare is permeating our world. This is what Jesus was referring to:

- There are five signs that Jesus spoke about that are in the world, continuing and even worsening today. They are found in verses 4-8 of Matthew 24. Those five signs are false christs, wars and rumors of wars, famine, plagues, and earthquakes. Although these signs have appeared throughout history, they have increased exponentially as the world has seemed to grow more dangerously aggressive and evil.

- When you carefully read this chapter, you discover further that sin is all around us. Sin is abounding and is vividly mentioned in Matthew 24:9-12. These sins are explained by Jesus and are described as murder, hatred, betrayal, deception, and a lack of love.

- Naturally, all of these signs and the sin that is running rampant throughout the world point to the second coming of Christ. The second coming is found in this same chapter of Matthew 24:27-31. It is mentioned twice in these verses. The first time it uses the Greek word *parousia* for the second coming of Christ mentioned in verse 27. The second time it uses the Greek word *erchomai* for the second coming mentioned in verse 30.

Note that two different Greek words are used for both times the second coming of Christ is mentioned in that chapter. Why are there two different Greek words used here for the second coming of Christ, just a few verses apart? Apparently the early translators and expositors viewed a difference of emphasis between the two times that it mentions the second coming.

The word *parousia* in verse 27, which means the coming or arrival of Christ, also refers to His "presence," or "to be near." From that word "coming" meaning "presence," or "to be near," we can understand the "catching away" of the saints, when the church meets the Lord in the air.[10] The word *erchomai* in verse 30, which means the coming of Christ, but in a more literal sense, means to "arrive," "make an appearance," or "come before the public."[11]

It is believed that the first mention of His coming in verse 27 refers to the removal of the church from this earth, and the second mention of the second coming found in verse 30 is the literal return of Christ when He sets foot on the earth at the end of the tribulation. The tribulation is placed in verse 29 between those two references. Placed in this order, you have the removal of the church from this earth in verse 27, the great tribulation in verse 29, and the literal second coming of Christ in verse 30.

That word *parousia* found in Matthew 24:27 is exactly the same Greek word that is used in 1 Thessalonians 4:15 when it refers to Christ's coming in verses 13-18 referring to the "catching away" of the church. In that same chapter, we see that in 1 Thessalonians 4:17, there is another Greek word that I believe proves that there is a removal of the church from this earth. We know that the word "rapture" is not found in the Bible, but the word "caught up" is. In that verse, we read:

> Then we which are alive and remain shall be caught up together...in the clouds, to meet the Lord in the air: and so shall we ever be with the Lord (1 Thessalonians 4:17 KJV).

10. Thayer and Smith, Greek Lexicon entry for Parousia, The KJV New Testament Greek Lexicon, accessed August 9, 2013, http://www.biblestudytools.com/lexicons/greek/kjv/parousia.html.
11. Thayer and Smith, Greek Lexicon entry for Erchomai, The KJV New Testament Greek Lexicon, accessed August 9, 2013, http://www.biblestudytools.com/lexicons/greek/kjv/erchomai.html.

The words "caught up" in verse 17 is the Greek word *harpazo,* and it means "to seize, carry off by force, to snatch out, or away."[12] It is the same word used in Acts 8:39 to describe Philip being caught away after witnessing to the Ethiopian eunuch. It is used when the apostle Paul was caught up into the third heaven, or paradise, in 2 Corinthians 12:2-4. It is also the same word used in Revelation 12:5 to describe the young child being caught up to God to escape the evil hand of the Dragon, who is described as the Devil.

Truly, Christ is going to remove the church from this world as a distinct action separate from His literal coming when he fights the battle of Armageddon and set up His kingdom on this earth. Many people try to say that those who believe in the rapture are escapists, hoping for a way out. But it is a perfect view of the continued spiritual warfare as we approach the second coming of Christ.

The removal of the church is similar to other instances in the Bible in which people have been removed at certain times. As examples:

1. Enoch escaped death and the evil of the pre-flood world by being translated to heaven.

2. Noah and his family were saved from the flood.

3. Lot was delivered from the evils of Sodom and Gomorrah.

4. The second coming of Christ depicts "one shall be taken, and the other left."

The chaotic time in which we are living since the turn of the twenty-first century has been a time of uncertainty filled with rage and violence. It has been a time of turmoil, popular uprisings, revolutions, social turbulence, and clashes. Again, this is all a part of the spiritual warfare that the nations are involved with because the Devil has been in a rage, trying to reverse the rebirth of the nation of Israel. While we have had these kinds of disturbances for centuries, it has been the volume of these disturbances and the ferocity of their impact that is preparing the world

---

12. Thayer and Smith, Greek Lexicon entry for Harpazo, The KJV New Testament Greek Lexicon, accessed August 9, 2013, http://www.biblestudytools.com/lexicons/greek/kjv/harpazo.html.

for the end of evil and the beginning of the reign of Christ. The climax of the end times will reverberate louder and stronger than at any other point in history.

The revolutions that we have seen in the beginning of this century in governments all around the world are preparing for the ten-toed kingdom as seen in Nebuchadnezzar's dream in Daniel 2. Nebuchadnezzar dreamed about a statue that had a head of gold, breast and arms of silver, thighs of brass, legs of iron, and feet of iron and clay. While the world has been living out the history of that statue through the nations that have been in power for centuries, these 10 toes of iron and clay are reserved for the time of the great tribulation in the end times. They are a picture of the ten nations that will be led by the Antichrist during that time. We read in Daniel about this great image that Nebuchadnezzar dreamed:

> Whereas you saw the feet and toes, partly of potter's clay and partly of iron, the kingdom shall be divided; yet the strength of the iron shall be in it, just as you saw the iron mixed with ceramic clay. And as the toes of the feet were partly of iron and partly of clay, so the kingdom shall be partly strong and partly fragile. As you saw iron mixed with ceramic clay, they will mingle with the seed of men; but they will not adhere to one another, just as iron does not mix with clay. And in the days of these kings the God of heaven will set up a kingdom which shall never be destroyed; and the kingdom shall not be left to other people; it shall break in pieces and consume all these kingdoms, and it shall stand forever (Daniel 2:41-44).

The kingdoms at the time of the end will be weak, fragile, and ineffective because the kingdoms of that time will not be cohesive. The rebellions of the Middle East and other parts of the world are carrying out that kind of government, and are preparing the world for a government headed by the Antichrist that will be too weak to last long. Just as the iron and clay would not mix in that dream of Nebuchadnezzar's, so the future governments of the time of the great tribulation will fall apart when Christ returns to the earth at the end of the tribulation. His return is pictured as a great stone that comes from a mountain and fills the entire earth. In just such a way, His government will fill the entire earth during the millennium.

That ten kingdom government of the Antichrist will be strong for a while, but will tear apart and make way for the government headed by Christ. The unrest and crises that we have seen at the beginning of this century in Tunisia, Yemen, Iraq, Libya, Algeria, Bahrain, Saudi Arabia, Syria, Egypt, and Iran are only a tip of the iceberg when compared with the turmoil of the future time of the great tribulation. This unrest reveals democracy fighting against autocracy, or dictatorship. They are two ideologies that won't mix, but will be the basis of the weak kingdoms that will rule with the Antichrist during the great tribulation.

America is one of the three great superpowers that came out of World War II along with England and the USSR. Just as England and the USSR lost their superpower status so America is losing hers. We have been one of the great global powers since the end of the great wars, but now that status is collapsing. We are collapsing for the five major reasons mentioned in the previous chapter, but not to worry: God has all things under control!

The immorality in America is growing at a feverish pace. The culture is set against biblical precepts, and that immorality has become so embedded in our society that it seems as if nothing can turn it around. America has gotten away from its biblical foundation. It is playing with the fires of change and destruction; and at some future time will no longer be the mighty superpower that it once was. Other nations in history have proved that over and over again.

We have been the global policeman for decades, but now that is changing. True, we are still a great power, but all powers of the past have collapsed, no matter how powerful they were. Seemingly at a moment's notice, we can have our troops in any part of the world, but just as other great powers of history have gone beyond a military point that is out of their control, we too will suffer with the winds of change. In our case, it will be with the winds of anti-Americanism, antiwar, antimilitary, and anti-involvement. We will slide into an era of, at least partial, isolationism from the rest of the world.

Additionally, global economic depression is just as sure to happen as the Great Depression of 1929. Worldwide economic depression, or economic change, will be a necessary occurrence in order for the coming Antichrist to offer his brand of solutions for the worldwide crisis. In 2008, America and the world had a deep economic shaking that has left numerous nations on the verge of economic collapse. Even though there have been periods of recovery, this type of event sometime in the future will be a prelude to the coming crisis that will happen in order for the appearance of the Antichrist to take place. The financial solution offered under the powerful and fearful control of the Antichrist:

> And that no man might buy or sell, save he that had the mark, or the name of the beast, or the number of his name (Revelation 13:17 KJV).

With that in mind, we must remember that the primary battle in spiritual warfare is between God and the Devil. It's not between you and the Devil; it's between God and the Devil. Our smaller battle is but a part of the larger picture of the battle between the two of them. What we need to do is be supportive in praise and prayer toward God, and rest in the victory that God has given to us. The Devil has wanted the worship and praise that rightfully belongs to God, and we are the ones who determine that. That is the core of spiritual warfare.

Remember also that God has completed the laws of purpose and accomplishment in our lives. Those laws include power over Satan and the will to live exclusively for God; spiritual rest and an intuitive response of love toward God; all the spiritual blessings that are afforded to us in God's Word; and the material and economic blessings given to God's people despite the economic havoc that has been created by the greed of this world. Remember too, as we bless others, we reap the blessing of God in our lives in all areas of our relationship with Him.

Finally, God is going to gather the nations of the world together for the battle of Armageddon. This is what it says in Joel 3:2 and Zechariah

14:2. His Son, Jesus Christ, will return to the earth, but He will not fight against Islam, Buddhism, Hinduism, or any other religion. He will fight against the nations of the world. Today, there are politicians, newscasters, school leaders, and even some ministers who make a big deal about the new perceptions on the separation of church and state, a concept very different from our founding fathers' view of the separation of church and state. In the end, they'll get their wish. At Armageddon, the church and state will indeed be separate because the church will be returning from heaven with Christ, and it will make war on the nations of the world. In essence, it will be the church against the state with Christ and the church winning as the nations of the world are defeated! Then in the millennium, Christ will rule in a theocratic government as Israel and the church will rule over the nations with Him.

PRAYER FOR THE NATIONS

Referring back to the book of Daniel, the angel Gabriel told Daniel about the long time that was appointed for the end times so he went into fasting and prayer. For twenty-one days he prayed for Israel and the changes coming to the nations. His prayer was during the winding down of the great superpower, Babylon, and the rising of the next, Persia. The messenger that came to him from God told Daniel about the power struggle he was having with the "prince" of Persia. This "prince" was a picture of the classic struggle mentioned by Paul in the New Testament where he writes that our struggle is with "principalities and powers, against the rulers of the darkness of this world, against spiritual wickedness in high places." In Daniel's case, this prince was part of the ruling "powers" over the nation of Persia.

Unbeknownst to Daniel, his prayer was right in the midst of this great superpower change. This messenger told Daniel about the things that would befall the nation of Israel in the latter days. Then the messenger told him that the next "prince" he was to struggle with was the "prince of Greece," the next superpower that was to come to the scene.

Intergalactic Warfare

So too, with the winding down of America as a great superpower, what we need to do is pray for America as Daniel did for Israel in Daniel 9 and 10. His prayer and confession on behalf of the nation of Israel sounds like a prayer that we should be able to pray for the United States of America. At this point, prayer for America is critical for its survival. We also need to pray for the nations of the world as well.

Every day we should tap into the power source of prayer. We should pray about the struggles of the nations of the world, as well as the terrorism, hatred, and war that exists today. There are ruling principalities and powers that exist today over all nations, and we need to pray God's will in every situation. Prayer is an integral part of knowing what our part should be and how we can zero in on what God wishes to do with the nations; He can reveal His great and marvelous plans to us, His people.

> But there is a God in heaven who reveals secrets, and He has made known to King Nebuchadnezzar what will be in the latter days (Daniel 2:28).

> Surely the Lord God does nothing, unless He reveals His secret to his servants the prophets (Amos 3:7).

This is where you and I have to step up to the plate. The reliance of God upon us is of paramount importance. He has dictated and established the avenues of prayer that we need to be involved in, and has told us the impact it can have on Him as He moves His hand over the nations. It is vital that we discover what His will is for the nations, so that we can be of valuable service for His work around the world. It is at this point that we pray into His will. How do we pray His will to be done, and what should we pray about? We can discover how to pray His will by continually citing the line from the Lord's Prayer that says, "Thy will be done on earth as it is in heaven." As we keep praying His will to be done, He can hear our prayer and answer our prayer. When we pray for the world, we should pray:

1. For the leaders of the nations.

2. That the gospel will have an impact on the nations and be preached in the entire world.

3. For laborers to be sent into the harvest field so that souls will be saved.

4. That healings will take place.

5. For financial blessings to be poured out on God's people.

6. That individuals and church worship services will be filled with the Holy Spirit.

7. That a powerful awareness of the soon return of the Lord Jesus Christ as Messiah and King will have a profound effect on the entire world and on all religions.

Again, God has all things under His control despite all of the chaos in the world today. Despite the political confusion, despair, revolution, and economic crisis, God still cares for you and is there to meet your needs. You may have lost your job or the value of your retirement savings, but the tough economic times are not focused on you. It is all centered on a global shift of superpower status back to the regions of the world that are the hotbed of historical battles of hatred and competitiveness. The areas of Europe, the Middle East, and the Far East are getting ready for the end times. The Devil may win some battles, but it is God who wins the war!

Let us fight the good fight of spiritual warfare. Let's get involved with prayer and praise so that God is continually honored in our families, our churches, and our nation. Let us be a part of the deciding factor in who wins the wars of this world. Let us do battle with the principalities and powers in the air so that there is a greater influence for the good, and not the evil. Let us remember that it is God who wins the final victory in the end of times. The Christian church should live in victory. The Bible gives to us these promises:

> Behold, I give unto you power to tread on serpents and scorpions, and over all the power of the enemy: and nothing shall by any means hurt you (Luke 10:19 KJV).

> We are more than conquerors through Him that loved us
> (Romans 8:37 KJV).

> Now thanks be unto God, which always causeth us to
> triumph in Christ (2 Corinthians 2:14 KJV).

> For whatsoever is born of God overcometh the world:
> and this is the victory that overcometh the world, even
> our faith (1 John 5:4 KJV).

Finally, 1 Thessalonians 5:1-4 says that the Lord is coming as a "thief in the night." It also says that He won't be coming for us as a "thief" because we are children of the "light" and not of the "night." The promise of Christ's coming for the church is quite different and quite dramatic because the believing church will be ready! Are you ready for the return of the Lord Jesus Christ to this earth? Are you anxiously waiting for the Lord to bring deliverance to His people? Are you continually praying for your loved ones to be saved? Are you praying for our nation that God will send a revival?

One day the Lord is coming for His people and we will forever be with the Lord.

> For the Lord Himself will descend from heaven with a
> shout, with the voice of an archangel, and with the trumpet
> of God. And the dead in Christ will rise first. Then we who
> are alive and remain shall be caught up together with them
> in the clouds to meet the Lord in the air. And thus we shall
> always be with the Lord. Therefore comfort one another
> with these words (1 Thessalonians 4:16-18).

> EVEN SO, COME LORD JESUS!

About the Author

A graduate of Zion (Northpoint) Bible College in Haverhill, MA with a bachelor's degree in Bible, David Siriano has been a minister for over fifty years, serving as a pastor and a speaker on biblical prophecy in seminars nationwide. He and his wife, Elsa May, travel and minister together. David has an avid interest in eschatology—the study of end time events—and has devoted over forty years to studying and teaching on it. As a social eschatologist, he has conducted numerous seminars on how the message of the Bible relates to the news events of today. He specializes in the biblical apocalyptic books of Daniel and Revelation, the Old Testament tabernacle, and those of the major and minor prophets. He is a college guest lecturer at Northpoint Bible College in Haverhill, MA, and is an adjunct professor at Crossroads Community International Bible Institute in East Hartford, CT.

He and his wife have been married fifty years and reside in West Henrietta, NY. They have two children, David Jr. and Darla, who are both involved in Christian ministry: David at The Church of North Orlando in Florida, and Darla at Faith Temple in Rochester, NY. They are blessed with eight grandchildren.

To contact David for speaking engagements, please email desir63@aol.com.

More Titles by 5 Fold Media

The Transformed Life
by John R. Carter
$20.95
ISBN: 978-1-936578-40-5

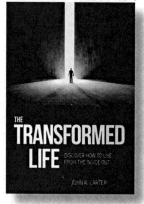

Personal transformation requires radical change, but your life will not transform until you change the way you think. Becoming a Christian ignites the process of transformation.

In this book, John Carter will teach you that God has designed a plan of genuine transformation for every person, one that goes far beyond the initial moment of salvation. More than a book, this 10 week, 40 day workbook will show you how to change.

Psalms: Poetry on Fire
The Passion Translation
by Brian Simmons
$19.00
ISBN: 978-1-936578-28-3

The ancient Psalms find the words that express our deepest and strongest emotions. They will turn your sighing into singing and your trouble into triumph. *The Passion Translation* of *The Psalms* will leave you amazed as the inspired words of Scripture unlock your heart to the wonder and glory of God's Word. It truly is Poetry on Fire!

I highly recommend this new Bible translation to everyone.
~ Dr. Ché Ahn, Senior Pastor of HRock Church in Pasadena, CA

Like 5 Fold Media on Facebook, follow us on Twitter!

*"To Establish and
Reveal"*
For more information
visit:
www.5foldmedia.com

Use your mobile device to scan
the tag above and visit our
website.
Get the free app:
http://gettag.mobi

CPSIA information can be obtained
at www.ICGtesting.com
Printed in the USA
FFOW01n2019040814
6690FF